A GENTLE AND QUIET SPIRIT

TRIBUTE

The most formal Festschrifts are limited to academic essays in honor of a fellow academician. Heritage Christian University Press takes a less formal approach; it is our heart's intent to recognize deserving servants of God within our staff and faculty. Barbara Dillon is a devoted and faithful coworker. Her diligence, consistency, character, and service merit every good word within this volume. For 23+ years, Barbara has blessed International Bible College/Heritage Christian University in numerous capacities. She has worked in childcare, in advancement, and as university receptionist.

Fittingly, this encouraging collection of essays covers an impressive breadth of informative, educational, practical, and contemplative topics. While some could assert that the primary beauty of a quiet and gentle spirit is its simplicity, we assert that depth of faith and spiritual awareness underlie that spirit. These are not merely human attributes and practices. They flow from and stand near the heart of God. They are the very essence of a Christ-honoring life.

Barbara is the daughter of a preacher. Both her husband Kevin and their son Richard are gospel preachers. And she is a natural-born servant. It is Barbara's inclination to look for ways to bless, yet she never seeks attention or recognition. She just continually does what is right, best, and needed with humility, grace, and quiet dignity. Barbara exhibits a joyful enthusiasm that is founded on her trust in the Lord she lovingly serves.

It honors Heritage Christian University to present this series of essays in honor of our friend and colleague Barbara Dillon. May her excellent example be appreciated and imitated by all who wear the name of Christ.

A GENTLE AND QUIET SPIRIT

A FESTSCHRIFT FOR BARBARA ANN DILLON

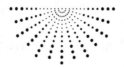

EDITORS OF HERITAGE CHRISTIAN UNIVERSITY PRESS

HERITAGE
CHRISTIAN UNIVERSITY
PRESS

Copyright © 2023 by Editors of Heritage Christian University Press

Cataloging-in-Publication Data

A gentle and quiet spirit: a Festschrift for Barbara A. Dillon / by editors of Heritage Christian University Press.

p. cm. (Heritage Legacy Series).

Includes Scripture index.

ISBN 978-1-956811-193 (hbk); 978-1-956811-20-9 (ebook)

1. Bible—Criticism, interpretation, etc. 2. Bible—Biography. 2. Elders (Church officers). I. Dillon, Barbara Ann, 1956-. II. Title. III. Series

081—dc20

Library of Congress Control Number: 2022923902

Cover design by Brad McKinnon and Brittany Vander Maas.

For more information:

Heritage Christian University Press
PO Box HCU
3625 Helton Drive
Florence, AL 35630

www.hcu.edu/publications

CONTENTS

Enjoy time at the 2019 Her-Stir

Singing soprano in chapel in the old Mars Hill Church of Christ building.

Helping serve food.

LIST OF CONTRIBUTORS

Bill Bagents is professor of ministry, counseling and Biblical studies at Heritage Christian University, Florence, Alabama, USA.

Laura S. Bagents is a classroom teacher who has taught children's Bible classes in local congregations and adjunct courses at Heritage Christian University, Florence, Alabama, USA.

Briana Butler is Associate Vice President of Marketing and Communications at Heritage Christian University, Florence, Alabama, USA.

Jamie Cox is Director of Library Services at Heritage Christian University, Florence, Alabama, USA.

Ed Gallagher is Professor of Christian Scripture at Heritage Christian University, Florence, Alabama, USA.

Michael Jackson is Associate Director of the Commission on Accreditation of the Association of Biblical Higher Education, Orlando, Florida, USA.

Debbie May is a former member of the board of directors at Heritage Christian University, Florence, Alabama, USA.

Melissa McFerrin is the Executive Administrative Assistant to the President at Heritage Christian University, Florence, Alabama, USA.

Autumn Richardson is Director of Distance Learning at Heritage Christian University, Florence, Alabama, USA.

Coy D. Roper is a retired professor from Heritage Christian University, Florence, Alabama, USA.

Dianne Tays is the business office clerk at Heritage Christian University, Florence, Alabama, USA.

Thomas Tidwell is an elder and preacher at the South Cobb church of Christ, and the Director of the Marietta Campus of Georgia School of Preaching and Biblical Studies in Marietta, Georgia, USA.

BIBLE ABBREVIATIONS

Old Testament

Gen	Genesis
Exod	Exodus
Lev	Leviticus
Num	Numbers
Deut	Deuteronomy
Josh	Joshua
Judg	Judges
Ruth	Ruth
1–2 Sam	1–2 Samuel
1–2 Kgs	1–2 Kings
1–2 Chr	1–2 Chronicles
Ezra	Ezra
Neh	Nehemiah
Esth	Esther
Job	Job
Ps	Psalms

Prov	Proverbs
Eccl	Ecclesiastes
Song	Song of Solomon
Isa	Isaiah
Jer	Jeremiah
Lam	Lamentations
Ezek	Ezekiel
Dan	Daniel
Hos	Hosea
Joel	Joel
Amos	Amos
Obad	Obadiah
Jonah	Jonah
Mic	Micah
Nah	Nahum
Hab	Habakkuk
Zeph	Zephaniah
Hag	Haggai
Zech	Zechariah
Mal	Malachi

New Testament

Matt	Matthew
Mark	Mark
Luke	Luke
John	John
Acts	Acts
Rom	Romans
1–2 Cor	1–2 Corinthians
Gal	Galatians
Eph	Ephesians
Phil	Philippians
Col	Colossians
1–2 Thess	1–2 Thessalonians
1–2 Tim	1–2 Timothy
Titus	Titus
Phlm	Philemon
Heb	Hebrews
Jas	James
1–2 Pet	1–2 Peter
1–2–3 John	1–2–3 John
Jude	Jude
Rev	Revelation

1
MARY MAGDALENE

DEBBIE MAY

God planned for women to become a part of Jesus's ministry on earth. His will for their lives included them giving of themselves to benefit the spread of the gospel in a much different way than the ways of His apostles. This would have been quite a task for the women of their time. Since the household and family duties fell to them, providing for and serving a group of men was no quick or easy work.

In one way or another, Jesus showed certain women who he was—the Messiah, Jesus Christ. And because of this, they sacrificed their time, comfort, and possessions to follow and provide for Him. Although that could not have been effortless or easy, they knew His life was more important.

We know from the New Testament gospels that Mary Magdalene was one of the women who followed Jesus. Apparently she was a woman of independent means, for she accompanied Jesus during His ministry and supported Him out of her own resources (Mark 15:40–41; Matt 27:55–56; Luke 8:1–3; John 19:25).

While it's not too far-fetched to assume that all of the women close to Jesus had an impact and influence in His life, as well as the lives of others, Mary Magdalene seemed to be one of His most trusted followers.

She had to have had a stigma or "reputation" after living with seven demons running around in her body and soul. But, after meeting Jesus, when people saw her living a normal life, providing for and serving the man who healed her, it had to have been such an emotional and intense testimony. She must have had amazing and wonderful stories to share with friends and others who were curious about this Jesus from Galilee. She knew Him, served Him, and was able to share His story in a way no one else could.

She sacrificed.

She served.

She influenced.

And it was all done in love.

When Mary Magdalene "saw that the stone had been removed from the entrance" (John 20:1), she rushed to Jerusalem and convinced Peter and John to go see the empty tomb. Rather than going to (in our mind) "lesser" disciples she went "right to the top." Peter and John must have respected her, because they immediately went with her (John 20:3–4).

Before returning to his heavenly home, Jesus had a task for Mary Magdalene. He told her to go to the others and tell them, "I am returning to my Father and your Father, to my God and your God" (John 20:17). She could do this because she was privileged to have seen him with her own eyes and heard Him speak with her own ears. When she proclaimed, "I have seen the Lord!" (John 20:18) it had to have been with a believable fervor and a sense of wonder.

If God's plan was indeed for women to play a part in Jesus's life on earth and to spread the gospel to others in their own way, let's look at some attributes of a godly woman. A godly woman distinguishes herself from the world by her self-control. She does not give free rein to emotions, attitudes, words, and appetites that are less than appropriate. She tries to control her thoughts to make them obedient to Christ (2 Cor 10:5). She attempts to control her emotions, rather than allowing them to control her. She controls her appetites and doesn't display an unrestrained passion for food and drink. She also controls her tongue. Her speech encourages, rather than tears down with idle gossip. She does not allow profanity and "unwholesome talk" to come out of her mouth (Eph 4:29). She also does her best to be of "noble character" and seeks to follow the example set by the virtuous woman in Proverbs 31:10–31. It seems to me that Mary Magdalene attempted to meet those goals, influenced others and spread the gospel as much as she could—and, was rewarded with a close relationship with Jesus. How much more could we ask than to have a relationship with Him that comes close to that?

How do you influence others for Jesus?

2
A CONTEMPLATION ON FAITHFUL QUIETNESS

BILL AND LAURA S. BAGENTS

I f our minds are biblically tuned, we love faithful quietness. Every time we see it, we're impressed and intrigued. How did this happen? How did this person gain such depth of faith and spirit? Why do I still have so far to go? Do the quiet ones realize how their example shines in its uniqueness? Do they know how impressive and challenging they are to those of us who want to follow them? Could they teach us if we asked? If so, would they need words? To what degree would the learning process flow from observation and imitation? Are some born with a disposition toward faithful quietness, or can God teach that virtue to anyone who's willing?

Perhaps another question must precede the ones above: What do we mean by "faithful quietness"? In its ultimate form, it's described in Isaiah 53:7–8, which says of God's suffering servant

He was oppressed, and he was afflicted, yet he opened not his mouth: like a lamb that is led to the slaughter, and like a sheep that before its shearers is silent, so he opened not his mouth.

It was perfectly embodied by our Lord during His life in the flesh (John 19:8–11, Luke 23:9, Mark 14:61 and 15:3–5, Matt 27:12–14).

Faithful quietness, as described in 1 Peter 2:18–25, is faith-filled imitation of Christ's example, following "in his steps." It includes

- Putting "away all malice and all deceit, and hypocrisy and envy and all slander" (1 Pet 2:1).
- Consistently living as "a chosen race, a royal priesthood, a holy nation, a people for his own possession" (1 Pet 2:9 and 12).
- Abstaining "from the passions of the flesh, which wage war against your soul" (1 Pet 2:11).
- Being "subject for the Lord's sake to every human institution" (1 Pet 2:13).
- Putting "to silence the ignorance of foolish people" by living in keeping with God's truth and Christ's character (1 Pet 2:17 with 2:11–12).
- Graciously enduring wrong and choosing to do right, no matter what others do (1 Pet 2:18–21).
- Foregoing both vengeance and demanding one's rights (1 Pet 2:22–25, Rom 12:19–21).
- Utterly entrusting ourselves "to him who judges justly" (1 Pet 2:23).

- Choosing incorruptible spiritual beauty and substance over appearance and posturing (1 Pet 3:1–6).
- Deserving or not, treating everyone with respect and compassion (1 Pet 3:7–12).

For followers of Jesus, faithful quietness is summarized by Galatians 2:20:

> I have been crucified with Christ. It is no longer I who live, but Christ who lives in me. And the life I now live in the flesh I live by faith in the Son of God, who loved me and gave himself for me.

Everything is by Him, for Him, through Him, under His authority, and to His glory. Everything we think, say, do, and desire flows from our love for Him and our trust that He is saving us.

THE CHOICE OF QUIETNESS

It would be hard to argue that Lamentations isn't the Bible's darkest book. The title itself offers a major clue. Yet within this painful book are amazing rays of heavenly light. Few shine as brightly as Lamentations 3:25–27.

> The Lord is good to those wait for him, to the soul who seeks him. It is good that one should wait quietly for the salvation of the Lord. It is good for a man that he bear the yoke in his youth.

The faithful of Jeremiah's day did not choose the yoke of bondage that plagued them. They were victims of a corrupt system created and maintained by self-serving leaders and many evil followers who just went along. The faithful of Jeremiah's day had no way to stop God's righteous judgment on their nation. Even the prayers of Moses and Samuel could not change the outcome (Jer 15:1). Even the presence of Noah, Daniel, and Job could not stop the coming destruction (Ezek 14:14).

The faithful could not stop the invasions, the siege, the devastation, and the deportation, but God allowed them an amazing choice—the ability to choose how they would endure those inevitable horrible events. They could choose to "wait quietly for the salvation of the Lord." They could choose to "bear the yoke" in faith, learning its lessons and welcoming the ways God would use it to shape them. They could choose to see a degree of good in the end of the world as they knew it. In the face of the unthinkable—including the destruction of God's temple— they could choose faith and hope. Jeremiah 30:10–11a reads,

> Then fear not, O Jacob my servant, declares the Lord, nor be dismayed, O Israel; for behold, I will save you from far away, and your offspring from the land of their captivity. Jacob shall return and have quiet and ease, and none shall make him afraid. For I am with you to save you, declares the Lord.

The question was (and is) never "Will the hard times

come?" THE QUESTION was (and always will be), "In a world of loss and woe, will we hold on to the promises of God?" Will we shape our attitudes and conduct by our knowledge of God's power, love, and goodness? Will we choose to live in faithful quietness when those around us rage?

Are we overstating the level of choice that God affords us? Consider Psalm 131. Some Bibles offer the caption, "I have calmed and quieted my soul." 131:2 says in effect, "I won't overprocess. I'll reject worry. I won't pretend that somehow I can figure everything out so that it all makes sense." It expresses a commitment to let God be God because we will never be up to that task. Psalm 131:3 is brilliant: "But I have calmed and quieted my soul, like a weaned child with its mother, like a weaned child is my soul within me." The meaning is clear:

"There's been a process, and it hasn't been pain-free. But I've moved to the next phase of life, to the next level of understanding. I will not get stuck in the choice to fight reality. I will move forward by adjusting to and embracing God's reality."

At the spiritual level, that's the key to faithful quietness.

Many passages affirm the choice of faithful quietness. Ecclesiastes 4:6 does so inferentially and poetically: "Better is a handful of quietness than two hands full of toil and a striving after the wind." Isaiah 7:4 offers a direct command to King Ahaz as the kings of Israel and Syria were about to attack him: "Be careful, be quiet, do not fear, do not let your heart be faint because of these two smoldering stumps . . . ." Ahaz had far more choice of attitude and trust than most realize.

Isaiah contributes notably to our understanding of faithful quietness as a choice and a blessing. Decades before the die of God's judgment against Judah was cast, Isaiah faithfully proclaimed, "For thus says the Lord God the Holy One of Israel, 'In returning and rest you shall be saved; in quietness and in trust shall be your strength.'" Sadly, ancient Judah was unwilling to embrace this promise, but it was there to be embraced. God has never offered an empty promise. His ancient people put their trust in false prophets, corrupt leaders, military alliances, and the physical temple. And they found no calm, peace, quiet, or salvation. We love the powerful reminder of the steadfast connection between quietness and trust in God.

Isaiah 32 speaks of a coming king who will reign in righteousness. Though there will be major resistance,

> Then justice will dwell in the wilderness, and righteousness abide in the fruitful field. And the effect of righteousness will be peace, and the result of righteousness, quietness and trust forever. My people will abide in a peaceful habitation, in secure dwellings, and in quiet resting places (Isa 32:15–18).

Ancient Judah may have heard these words primarily in terms of a restoration of their nation after a period of captivity; their longer meaning has always been spiritual.

There's biblical linkage between righteous, justice, peace, and quietness. And what of trust per verse 17? It speaks of trust in the coming king, the righteous king, the King of Kings.

As we think of values and behaviors linked to quietness, we must not neglect Zephaniah 3. In a paragraph extoling Israel's joy and restoration, the prophet writes,

> Sing aloud, O daughter of Zion, shout, O Israel! Rejoice and exult with all your heart, O daughter of Jerusalem! For the Lord has taken away the judgment against you; he has cleared away your enemies. The King of Israel, the Lord, is in your midst; you shall never again fear evil. On that day it shall be said in Jerusalem: "Fear not O Zion, let not your hands grow weak. The Lord your God is in your midst, a mighty one who will save; he will rejoice over you with gladness; he will quiet you by his love; he will exult over you with loud singing" (Zeph 3:14–17).

What joy! What hope! God will save, remove fear, and bring joy. But the sweetest line is "He will quiet you by his love." And that tremendous blessing even comes with a song of celebration!

WHY WOULD ANYONE NOT PURSUE FAITHFUL QUIETNESS?

Obvious answers abound. For those who do not believe in God, the question will never be addressed. For those who do not trust the truthfulness of Scripture, there can be no standard by which to evaluate the question or confidence in the biblical calls for this holy pursuit. The voice of the world is LOUD, persistent, and pervasive. Many have come to prefer the din of constant distraction. The pursuit of calm, peace, and focus must seem infinitely boring. Some may reject the pursuit of a quiet mind/spirit as unbiblical, as belonging to Eastern religions, whether Zen or otherwise. We would argue that such thinking unfairly conflates biblical meditation (Ps 1, Phil 4:8, 1 Tim 4:15) with one of its opposites.

Some have never been invited to pursue quietness. They lack a frame of reference from which to consider that option. They don't even know that option exists. For others, it remains stunningly difficult to think and live on a level more advanced than the world around us. For many Christians, the world—at least its better aspects—is the standard (Rom 12:1–2, Col 3:1–11). No doubt some have attempted the pursuit but found it too difficult. They lacked the wisdom, knowledge, foresight, or support system to continue the effort.

The first line of Lamentations 3:25 may offer a deeper reason that some forego pursuit of a quiet and gentle spirit. "The Lord is good to those who wait for him, to the soul who seeks him." Waiting for the Lord—an essential aspect of a quiet spirit—isn't just waiting; it also includes continual seeking of God's grace and God's truth. It is genuine work and commitment. It includes unwavering hope in God's goodness and salvation. To wait quietly on the Lord is hardly a passive stance toward life. There's massive spiritual activity surrounding the choices to "fear not" and "wait quietly for the salvation of the Lord." And that activity isn't just internal. It includes helping other believers embrace that peaceful perspective as well.

NEW TESTAMENT COMMANDS TO SEEK FAITHFUL QUIETNESS

On the level of principle, the Sermon on the Mount has much to contribute. It's no stretch to link a quiet spirit with meekness (Matt 5:5). Both loving enemies and embracing an ethic of non-retaliation flow from a deeply God-centered heart (Matt 5:38–48). Matthew 6:1–18 subtly promotes the virtue of "quietness" as it warns— three times—against the temptation to seek public praise. As Matthew 6:25–34 argues against worry, it strongly advocates the advantages of a settled, quiet, and trusting heart. It's no leap to propose that those of a quiet and deep spirit are best prepared to forego both unbiblical judging and the ever-present danger of unfairly comparing ourselves to others (Matt 7:1–5).

Several passages more overtly prescribe quietness.

… Aspire to live quietly, and to mind your own affairs, and to work with your own hands, as we instructed you, so that you may walk properly before outsiders and be dependent on no one (1 Thess 4:11–12).

While certainly not a command to become silent and irrelevant (Matt 5:13–17), the passage warns against making oneself the center of attention as if the gospel depended on our personal charisma. Paul wanted the Thessalonian Christians—and us—to be people of depth and substance, to be people of good reputation and trustworthy character. This message is strongly confirmed by 2 Thessalonians 3:11–12.

1 Timothy 2:1–10 also guides our thinking. A key reason Paul urges

> supplications, prayers, intercessions, and thanksgiving be made for all people [particularly] for kings and all who are in high positions [is so] that we may lead a quiet and peaceful life, godly and dignified in every way.

Such lives would strongly align with God's desire that "all people be saved and come to the knowledge of the truth." We are not denying the ancient truism, "The blood of the martyrs is the seed of the church." Rather we affirm that the gospel has equal saving power during times of calm and peace when it can be shared neighbor to neighbor. 1 Peter 4:13–17 speaks powerfully to this both—and nature of evangelism and the benefits of living in "good conscience" with "gentleness and respect."

In terms of direct affirmation, we are blessed to remember 1 Peter 3:1–6, the text from which this book takes its name. We pay extra attention when anything is described as "very precious" in God's sight. And that is exactly how the text describes "the imperishable beauty of a gentle and quiet spirit." It's the very spirit demonstrated by the Lord Himself (Matt 11:29).

BIBLICAL EXAMPLES OF QUIET SERVICE

In addition to Jesus, what other examples of a gentle and quiet spirit stand out in Scripture? We think of Rebekah, who was "very attractive in appearance" (Gen 24:16), but equally attractive in attitude and spirit. Her politeness and acts of service gained the attention of Abraham's servant and led to her place in the lineage of David and of Christ.

We think of Esther. Ultimately, her queenly service was anything but quiet, but God chooses to remind us of her pleasing disposition and her humble decision to heed her adopted father's counsel (Esth 2:8–11). Even as she exposed Haman's plot and saved God's people, she did so with amazing restraint and decorum (Esth 5–6). She played—and never over-played—her crucial role in God's plan. Of course much the same can be said of Mordecai. With the possible exception of his unwillingness to bow to Haman, he is consistently presented as unselfishly blessing, serving, and protecting.

We think of the unnamed widow of Zarephath who acted against sight and common sense to bless the prophet Elijah (1 Kgs 17). As she acted in faith during stunningly severe famine, "The jar of flour was not spent, neither did the jar of oil become empty, according to the word of the Lord that he spoke through Elijah." Admittedly, this lady's life was not always quiet. She became quite direct when her son died, and God raised the boy. It's our best judgment that one purpose of this amazing story is to remind us that a quiet spirit often flows from a soul that has grown deep and bold.

We think of the unnamed servant-girl of 2 Kings 5:1–4. All she needed to exact revenge on her captors was to keep silent. Rather than withholding crucial information, she told her mistress of the prophet of God in Samaria and opened a door to healing.

From the New Testament, we think of Mary, mother of Jesus, and her cousin Elizabeth. We know Elizabeth only as wife of a priest, mother of the forerunner of Jesus, and encourager of Mary (Luke 1:39–45 and 57–60). We see Mary snatched from obscurity to a vital role in God's plan, and we stand amazed by her faith, humility, and willingness to serve. "Then Mary said, 'Behold I am the servant of the Lord; let it be to me according to your word'" (Luke 1:38). Mary's song of praise (Luke 2:46–55) stands as one of the most beautiful and dynamic prayers in all of Scripture. For centuries, scholars have called that prayer The Magnificat!

We think of Tabitha, aka Dorcas (Acts 9:36–42). The text describes her as "full of good works and acts of charity." We learn a bit later that she sewed profusely. Those she blessed were not content to leave her dead; neither was God. Peter was summoned, God acted, and her resurrection "became known throughout all Joppa, and many believed in the Lord."

We think of Lydia. Acts 16 presents her as a business-woman, a homeowner, and a person of means. As soon as she and her household were baptized, she insisted that Paul and his co-workers accept the hospitality of her house. Though that plan was delayed, her heart was in the right place. She showed a servant's heart.

In the broadest of terms, we think of Hebrews 11:32–
40. In terms of notoriety and public influence it's a mixed
text. It mentions Gideon, Barak, Samson, Jephthah, David
and Samuel by name. It mentions the prophets as a group
and Daniel without using his name (Heb 11:33). It
mentions people who conquered kingdoms and "put
foreign armies to flight." It includes "women [who]
received back their dead by resurrection." But it also
includes unnamed victims of mocking, flogging, chains,
imprisonment, and other afflictions. It adds those who
lost their lives to stoning and sword.

What do we find remarkable about Hebrews 11:32–
40? The named and the unnamed, the survivors and those
who died, those with major public impact and those who
died in obscurity—none are overlooked by God. All are
counted precious by God. All are equally described in the
phrase "of whom the world was not worthy." One need
not be famous to be beloved, honored, and appreciated by
God. The faithful who manifest a gentle and quiet spirit
stand as pillars in the kingdom. Their examples make us
better because they so beautifully honor God.

As we contemplate both biblical and current examples
of a quiet and faithful spirit—particularly the example of
Jesus Himself—we feel the pull of grace and opportunity.
We work to live up to the high calling of scripture. And
we welcome the ever-increasing influence of deeply spiritual brethren who consistently show us God's better way.
Because we must keep growing toward Jesus, we deepen
our commitment to trust God above all, especially above
ourselves.

ELDERS AS SHEPHERDS OF SUFFERING SAINTS

AN EXEGESIS OF 1 PETER 5:1–5

COY D. ROPER

A bbreviations used for Bible versions

JB   Jerusalem Bible

KJV   King James Version

NASB   New American Standard Bible

NIV   New International Version

NKJV   New King James Version

NRSV   New Revised Standard Version

RSV   Revised Standard Version

ELDERS AS SHEPHERDS OF SUFFERING SAINTS: AN EXEGESIS OF 1 PETER 5:1–5

When the saints are suffering, especially because of persecution, what should be done?[1] According to 1 Peter 5:1–5, part of the answer is that elders need to do their work correctly. That message is relevant today, not just because Christians may suffer, but because when a church follows the instructions of 1 Peter 5:1–5 it will be better equipped to face any crisis. The passage is also important to Churches of Christ because it addresses an issue which has troubled the church in recent years—namely, the authority of elders.

But before the message can be applied it must be understood in its own context.

BACKGROUND

But an understanding of the passage requires, first, a consideration of its background: In what circumstances was it written? How does the passage fit into the book?

Circumstances of writing

Who wrote 1 Peter, from where and when, to whom, and for what purpose?[2]

Author. The author claims to be the apostle Peter (1:1). Although this claim is sometimes rejected, or alternatives are sought for the view that Peter himself wrote the book

not long before his death in the seventh decade, this paper accepts the traditional view.[3]

Place and date. The place of writing is "Babylon" (5:13). It seems most likely that here, as in Revelation (see Rev 14:8; 17:2), Babylon is a code word for Rome.[4]

The date is thought to be in the late 50s to the middle 60s. Some reject this date because they believe the letter speaks of an empire-wide official persecution, and that never occurred until late in the first century (or even later). However, in 1 Peter the persecution is not necessarily

- empire-wide,
- instigated by the Roman government,
- fatal to Christians.[5]

Most likely the letter was written toward the end of Peter's career from Rome.

Recipients. The recipients were "exiles of the Dispersion in Pontus, Galatia, Cappadocia, Asia, and Bithynia" (1:1). Although the language speaks of a Jewish experience, it seems obvious that the recipients were predominantly Gentile Christians. Peter speaks of their former ignorance and idolatry (1:14; 4:3) and says that once they were "no people" (2:10). It is likely that in these churches there were both Jewish and Gentile Christians, with a majority of Gentiles.[6]

What caused Peter to write them? They were suffering.

Theme and purpose. The letter is about the suffering of

the saints.[7] The Greek word for "suffering," *pascho*, appears twelve times in the book,[8] more than in any other New Testament book.[9] Some word or idea related to suffering is found in about 24 of the 105 verses of the book.[10]

The recipients are told that they may have "to suffer various trials" (1:6) and that they will suffer "unjustly" (2:19), for "doing right" (2:20; 3:17), "for righteousness sake" (3:14), and "as a Christian" (4:16; 4:14).[11] They may be spoken against (2:12, 15) and their good behavior may be reviled (3:16), but they are assured that they will have to suffer only for "a little while" (5:10).[12] Christ's sufferings are also prominent. The prophets predicted them (1:11); when Christ suffered, He set an example (2:21–25); He suffered (or died)[13] unjustly (3:18); those who suffer remember (4:1) and "share Christ's suffering" (4:13), which Peter witnessed (5:1).

Peter at times seems to say only that these Christians may suffer (see 1:6; 2:12; 2:19, 20; 3:14–17; 4:14–16), even asserting that if they do right they are not likely to suffer (3:13), although they may (3:14). But he also says suffering is a certainty, speaking of a "fiery ordeal" (4:12) they are experiencing, warning of an approaching time of judgment (4:17; 5:9, 10),[14] and declaring that some Christians will suffer (4:19). He is not just writing about a theoretical possibility, but about a real problem.[15]

The origin of this persecution and suffering lies in the fact that "pagan culture frowned upon any break with ancestral tradition in matters of religion." If people changed their gods, it was feared that all kinds of evil would follow. "Given these fears, the larger society would attempt to enforce conformity and to prevent socially divergent behavior."[16]

Peter's purpose, therefore, is to help his readers to remain faithful in a time of suffering, to encourage them to "stand fast" in the "true grace of God" (5:12).[17]

Structure. How does 1 Peter 5:1-5 accomplish that purpose? The following outline of the book reveals that Peter follows the usual form of New Testament epistles, and, in the body of the letter, emphasizes what a church should do when its members are experiencing persecution and suffering.[18]

1:1-2—Salutation, naming the author and addressees.

1:3-5:11—The body of the letter can be divided into four major parts, plus a final admonition.

1:3-2:10—Part One: In a time of persecution and suffering, each Christian needs to remember his blessings.

1:1-2:3—Stresses individual blessings: "chosen," "sanctified" (1:2), "born anew" (1:3, 23), "ransomed" (1:18), "purified" (1:22), a Christian has "a living hope" (1:3), an "inheritance" (1:4), a "salvation" (1:5, 9; 2:2), and a "grace" (1:13) which await Christ's coming (1:5, 7, 13). He also has responsibilities (1:13-17, 22; 2:1, 2), but the emphasis is on the blessings.

In 2:4-10 the emphasis is on the blessings enjoyed by God's people as a group. They are a "spiritual house" (2:5), "a chosen race, a royal priesthood, a holy nation, God's own people," who are to declare God's wonderful deeds (2:9).

2:11-3:12—Part Two: In a time of persecution and

suffering, Christians need to do right in every relationship. The relationships are:

- 2:11, 12—The Christian to the world,
- 2:13–17—The Christian to government,
- 2:18–25—The slave to his master,
- 3:1–7—Husband and wife,
- 3:8–12—The Christian to all, especially to one another.[19]

3:13–4:19—Part Three: In a time of persecution and suffering, each Christian needs to react properly to suffering. They should:

- 3:14—Not be afraid,
- 3:15—Be prepared to defend their position,
- 3:16; 4:3, 4; 4:19—Keep a clear conscience,
- 4:1—Remember Christ's suffering,
- 4:7–11—Seek one another's good,
- 4:12–16—Not be surprised, but rejoice,
- 4:17–19—Trust in God.

5:1-5—Part Four: In a time of persecution and suffering, the leadership must function correctly. The elders must do their work properly (5:14). Others must respond to that leadership in the right way (5:5).

5:6-11—Final admonitions: trust in God (5:6, 7), resist the devil (5:8, 9), remember the hope of glory (5:10, 11).

5:12, 13—Closing, which tells by whom, from where,

and for what purpose the letter was written, and sends greetings.

EXPLANATION

To understand 1 Peter 5:1—5, it is necessary to examine its connection with the rest of the letter, and then to consider the instructions it gives to elders and others.

CONNECTION, TRANSITION

Why does Peter find it necessary to give instructions concerning elders when the saints are suffering? The answer lies in the fact that a suffering group gets its strength to survive from its solidarity. Elliot says,

> For the harassed Christian movement in Asia Minor to survive and grow, isolated pockets of believers throughout the provinces required a sense of the ties which bound them in a common cause. If Christians were to resist external pressures and be mutually supportive, a high degree of group consciousness was essential.[20]

Thus, although the letter describes the responsibilities of individual church members, it is also very concerned with the church as a group. Notice especially 2:9, 10, where their status as the people of God is emphasized; 4:8–11, where their responsibility to use their gifts for one another is pointed out; 4:17, where the "household of

God" is mentioned; 2:17 and 5:9, where "the brotherhood" is held in high regard; and 1:22 and 3:8, where mutual love is enjoined. First Peter does not advocate "Lone Ranger" Christianity, but encourages Christians to "stand fast" as members of congregations.

But if this is so, the role of the leaders of the congregations becomes very important. If they fail, the flock could be scattered and lost. Thus, as Peter nears the end of the epistle, he adds a word to and about the elders.

The specific connection between 5:1–5 and what goes before is an *oun* "therefore,"[21] at the beginning of the passage. This "therefore" may connect what follows with the fact that judgment is about to "begin with the household of God" (4:19).[22] But it should be noted that the subject of the sentence is "I" in "I exhort" (*parakalo*). It may be that Peter has the entire situation in mind when he says, "Because of all this, I exhort you … ." Thus, "therefore" may connect 5:1–5 not just to the verses immediately before, but to everything that precedes it.

INSTRUCTIONS TO ELDERS

Nevertheless, whatever the connection, the instructions concerning elders are plain. They can best be understood by asking and answering four questions.

Who were these elders? "Elders" can "indicate either the elderly … or be a name for church leaders."[23] In 5:1 it *is* used for a class of men who occupied an "official" capacity as leaders of local churches.[24] Each group of elders was to serve only their local congregation: "Tend the flock of

God that is your charge"(5:2).[25] It is interesting that Peter identifies himself as a "fellow-elder."[26] Many accept the view that Peter was an elder because he was an apostle; all apostles were elders.[27] But in light of the fact that the New Testament differentiates between apostles and elders (Acts 15:6, 22; Eph 4:11), this seems unlikely.[28]

Since there is no definite article preceding "elders" in the Greek text ("I exhort elders," rather than "I exhort the elders"), the writer may be speaking of the indefinite situation that prevailed in the churches: some congregations had elders, others did not. Michaels emphasizes this idea by translating, "To any elders among you, therefore, I appeal … ."[29] In New Testament times, churches existed for a period of time without elders (see Acts 14:23; Titus 1:5).

What were the elders to do? Peter gives them one task, with an explanatory note to help them understand that task.

That one task was to "tend the flock of God that is your charge" (5:2). The word for "tend" is the verb form of the word for shepherd; its meaning is "to act as a shepherd."[30] The use of this verb for the work of "elders" attests to the fact that in the New Testament the terms "elders" and "pastors" refer to the same work or "office" or men.

The idea of shepherding the flock would have tapped into a rich store of images. The readers knew the twenty-third Psalm, in which the Lord is spoken of as a shepherd. They probably knew that Jesus had said "I am the good shepherd" (John 10:11) and knew what He said He would do for the flock. Most likely, they were familiar with the story Jesus told about the shepherd searching for the lost sheep. Certainly they knew from this epistle that Christ was their shepherd (2:25 and 5:4). It was against this background that they would have understood their responsibility to "shepherd the flock."

Then, Peter further explains their responsibility by adding the expression "exercising the oversight."[31] The Greek word is *episkopountes*, a verb (participle) form related to the noun *episkopos*, which is translated as "overseer" or "bishop" in Acts 20:28 and Titus 1:1.[32] In shepherding the flock, the elders were to "act as overseers."

How were the elders to do their work?[33] After telling elders what to do, Peter tells them how to do it. The "how-to" instructions come in three pairs, dealing with, according to Calvin, three vices to which leaders are especially prone—"sloth, desire for gain, and lust for power."[34]

They were to do their job "not by constraint but willingly" (5:2). The elder should not have to be forced to do the work,[35] nor do his job "simply because he has been so appointed—and therefore halfheartedly—but from a real desire to serve."[36] Their work should be like that of "a volunteer who delights to do the work."[37]

They were to work "not for shameful gain but eagerly" (5:2). Elders were sometimes paid for their service,[38] and, in addition, they probably handled the church's money.[39] Those who were greedy thus had at least two ways to profit from their service. But, even if there was a chance of profit, they were to serve for some better reason, "eagerly," "with inward delight ... [with a] desire to serve [which would] precede any consideration of personal profit."[40] Or, as another put it, with "zeal, energy, and enthusiasm for the job."[41]

They were to shepherd the flock "not as domineering over those in your charge but being examples to the flock" (5:3). This third requirement is probably intended to be the climax of the series.[42] In a time of persecution, elders might be especially tempted to rule with an iron hand "for the good of the church." But that is not how they are to lead; Grudem says that the word translated "domineering"

> means "forcefully ruling over, subduing", and can carry the nuance of a harsh or excessive use of authority ... . The word always seems to involve bringing something into subjection by the use of force, whether physical, military, or political. Here Peter forbids the use of arbitrary, arrogant, selfish, or excessively restrictive rule.[43]

In contrast, the elders are to lead by example, a concept found frequently in the New Testament.[44]

What would motivate the elders to do the work? Peter makes two appeals which he hopes will lead them to do what he asks, one implied and the other openly expressed.

First, he says, "I exhort the elders." The word "exhort" does not carry with it the connotation of "I command" or "I require,"[45] but suggests the idea of appeal or encouragement. Then Peter appeals on the basis of who he is in 5:1.[46] He is "a fellow elder."[47] He is one of them. He is a "witness of the sufferings of Christ." He was close to Christ and is acquainted with suffering.[48] He is a "partaker in the glory that is to be revealed." But his readers also will partake in that glory after they have suffered (1:5–9).

Who would not be inclined to listen to an apostle who appealed to, rather than commanded, them, and who shared their work, an insight into their suffering, and their hope?

The second motivation is appealed to directly by Peter in 5:4: "And when the chief Shepherd is manifested you will obtain the unfading crown of glory." If the elders are faithful as "undershepherds" they will be well rewarded with a crown of victory![49]

Instructions to the younger Next Peter provides instructions to another group: "Likewise[50] you that are younger be subject to the elders" (5:5a).[51] Who were these "younger ones" (*neoteroi*)? It is unlikely that this is to be linked closely with the "household code" found earlier in the letter, since the instructions here are not perfectly parallel with the passages in 2:18 and 3:1–7, and since the context here is the church, rather than the household. Furthermore, since it is certain that "elders" in 5:1 refers to "elders" in an "official" sense, it is likely that "elders" in 5:5 is used in the same way.[52] Who then are the "younger"? It could be those who are young in faith, in contrast to the elders, whose faith is more mature.[53] It could refer to all those in the church who are not elders.[54] Or it could speak of the younger members of the congregation.[55] In any case, what was their responsibility? To "be subject" to the elders; to follow their lead.[56]

Instructions to all Peter then concludes this section of

his letter by giving instructions to all his readers: "Clothe yourselves, all of you, with humility toward one another, for 'God opposes the proud, but gives grace to the humble'" (5:5b).[57] After informing the elders of their responsibilities and those who were young in the faith of their need to follow the elders' lead, Peter speaks to all— elders and younger ones and, most likely, any Christians not included in these two categories.

Why does he at this point speak specifically of the need of all to have "humility toward one another"? The answer may be that he wants to put a brake on the desire of any elders who might think that their followers' submission gave them permission to "lord it over" (KJV) the flock. Humility would eliminate arrogance and self-will, and produce service.[58]

The ideal, therefore, is for all Christians, including elders, to be humble, determined to serve as did their Master. In such a situation elders will see themselves as servants of the flock and others will gladly follow their lead.

Conclusion It is fair to say that if elders properly fulfilled the role God gave them, others submitted to their leadership, and all were "clothed with humility," churches and Christians would be more likely to "stand fast" in the faith than if these instructions were neglected.

APPLICATION

This passage obviously speaks to various needs in the church today:

- The need for elders.
- The need for elders to do their work correctly.
- The need for the "younger ones" to submit to the elders.
- The need for all Christians to put on humility towards all others.

But it also speaks to a controversy which is troubling the church: the issue of the authority of elders.[59] Some are unwilling to grant that elders have any authority.[60] On the other side are those who teach, in effect, that to reject the authority of elders is to reject the authority of God.[61]

First Peter 5:1–5 does not help the cause of those who say that elders have no authority. The requirement of the younger to "be subject to the elders" implies that the elders have authority, as do the terms used for them. The word "elder" would have carried with it the idea of authority to Peter's readers.[62] The idea of an "overseer" (*episkopos*) implied authority—an implication confirmed when the readers hear Christ spoken of as the *episkopon* (2:25; RSV: "Guardian") of their souls.[63] Similarly, the expression "shepherd" implied authority,[64] an idea confirmed by the designation of Christ as Shepherd (2:25; 5:4).[65]

Furthermore, the prohibition of "domineering" implies that the elders were, by virtue of being elders, in a position of authority which could be abused. Peter warns them, not against having authority, but against the abuse of authority.[66]

But neither does this passage provide comfort for

those who say that elders are to "rule with an iron hand." The passage tells them, not only that they are not to lead in a domineering way, but also that they are to act humbly toward their brethren. Thus, any inclination they might have to rule as dictators is eliminated.[67]

On the question of the authority of elders, therefore, 1 Peter 5:1–5 teaches that elders have authority, but are not to lead in an authoritative, domineering, manner.[68]

ENDNOTES

1. Christians are not called "saints" in 1 Peter, but are said to be "sanctified" (1:2, RSV; unless otherwise indicated, the RSV will be used for quotations).

2. Other introductory questions will not be addressed. The canonicity and unity of the text of 1 Peter are assumed. For recent introductions to the book see: J. Ramsey Michaels, *1 Peter*, in Word Biblical commentary. vol. 49 (Waco, TX: Word Books, 1988), xxxi–lxxv; Peter H. Davids, *The First Epistle of Peter*, in The New International Commentary on the New Testament. ed. F. F. Bruce (Grand Rapids, MI: Eerdmans), 3–44; John H. Elliot, "Peter, First Epistle of," in *The Anchor Bible Dictionary* (ABD), ed. David Noel Freedman, vol. 5 (New York: Doubleday, 1992), 269–278; R. P. Martin, "Peter, First Epistle of," in *The International Standard Bible Encyclopedia*. ed. Geoffrey W. Bromiley, vol. 3 (Grand Rapids, MI: Eerdmans, 1986), 802–815; D. A. Carson, Douglas J. Moo, and Leon Morris, *An Introduction to the New Testament* (Grand Rapids, MI: Zondervan, 1992), 421–431.

3. Representative of those who favor a pseudonymous author are Spencer [Richard A. Spencer, "Peter, Letters of," *Mercer Dictionary of the Bible,* ed. Watson E. Mills (Macon GA: Mercer University Press, 1990), 677–679 and Perrin and Duling (Norman Perrin and Dennis C. Duling, *The New Testament: An Introduction,* 2nd ed. (New York: Harcourt Brace Jovanovich, Inc., 1974, 1982), 377]. Among those who seek a relatively conservative alternative to the traditional view are: Elliot, *ABD* (277), Martin (808, 809), Michaels (lxi–lxvii), and Davids (3–7). In favor of the traditional viewpoint that Peter himself wrote the book in the 60s are: Carson, Douglas, and Moo, 422–424; Edwin A. Blum, "1 Peter," in *The Expositor's Bible Commentary,* ed. Frank E. Gaebelein, vol. 12 (Grand Rapids, MI: Zondervan, 1981), 210–212; Donald Guthrie, *New Testament Introduction,* 4th ed. (Downers Grove, IL: InterVarsity Press, 1990), 762–781; Everett F. Harrison, *Introduction to the New Testament,* rev. ed. (Grand Rapids, MI: Eerdmans, 1964, 1971), 403–407.

4. See Martin, 809; Davids, 10; Michaels, lxiii; et. al.

5. For the relevant scriptures in 1 Peter, see below under "Theme and Purpose." Peter speaks more of slander and abuse than of the likelihood of the Christian's dying for the faith. Elliot (*ABD,* 274), e.g., says that the persecution was "local, disorganized, and unofficial."

6. This is the "near consensus" of scholars today. Michaels, xlvi. See also: Davids, 8, 9; Spencer, 677; Carson, Douglas, Moo, 425; W. C. van Unnik, "Peter, First Letter of," *The Interpreter's Dictionary of the Bible,* ed.

George Arthur Buttrick, vol. 3 (Nashville: Abingdon, 1962), 761.

7. Harrison, 396, and Merrill C. Tenney, *The New Testament: Historical and Analytic Survey* (Grand Rapids, MI: Eerdmans, 1955), 359, 365.

8. Blum, 215.

9. *Young's Analytical Concordance to the Bible*, 22nd American ed., rev. ed. (Grand Rapids, MI: Eerdmans, n.d.).

10. In at least seventeen verses (Tenney [362] says sixteen), found in all five chapters, the book speaks of the suffering of Christians or predicts a time of suffering. In at least six verses the writer speaks of Christ's sufferings.

11. And when he says they should not return "evil for evil" (3:9), Peter implies that they will experience "evil."

12. Interestingly, though 5:8, 9 implies that the devil is the source of their suffering, it is clear that if Christians suffer it will be "according to God's will" (4:19; 3:17).

13. There is a textual question as to whether 3:18 should read "suffered" or "died." KJV and NKJV have "suffered;" RSV, NASB, NIV, NEB, and JB have "died." The difference is between *epathen* (from *pascho*) and *apethanen* (from *apothnskein*, to die). In contrast to the second edition which has *apethanen* the third edition of the United Bible Societies Greek New Testament includes *epathen* in the text as a "D" reading, indicating "a very high degree of doubt concerning the reading selected." Kurt Aland, et. al., eds., *The Greek New Testament*, 3rd ed. (New York: United Bible Societies, 1975), xiii (UBS[3]). For reasons for this change, see Bruce M. Metzger, *A Textual Commentary on the Greek New Testament* (New

York: United Bible Societies, 1971), 692, 693. Reflecting the newer Greek text, the NRSV has "suffered."

14. Michaels indicates that the words used in 4:12; 4:17; and 5:9 all suggest that the suffering is taking place at the time Peter writes. (Michaels, 260, 270, 302.)

15. The vacillation between "potential" and "actual" suffering is real, but it does not justify dividing the book into two documents. For an indication of the problem sometimes seen in this phenomenon, see, among others, Elliot, *ABD* (270), Martin (810), and Michaels (xxxviii –xxxix).

16. Charles H. Talbert, "Once Again: The Plan of 1 Peter," in *Perspectives on First Peter*, ed. Charles H. Talbert (Macon, GA: Mercer University Press, 1986), 145.

17. Black says, "Peter writes to encourage these Christians to remain faithful to the hope they have in Christ and to follow His example." Allen Black, Lecture, New Testament Exegesis, from class notes taken by Coy Roper (Harding University Graduate School of Religion, Memphis, TN, Summer, 1993).

18. Talbert, 141–151. For other outlines, see: Michaels (xxxvii), Davids (28, 29), Blum (218), Guthrie (800–804), Spencer (677), and Tenney (365).

19. This theme may continue through 3:13–17, which deals with the Christian's relationship to his persecutors.

20. John H. Elliot, *A Home for the Homeless* (Philadelphia: Fortress Press, 1981), 133. See also Davids (174).

21. The *oun* is missing from some ancient manuscripts but *is* found without comment in UBS[3]. Michaels (276) says it is "clearly original."

22. D. Edmond Hiebert, "Counsel for Christ's Under-Shepherds: An Exposition of 1 Peter 5:1–4," *Bibliotheca Sacra* 139 (1982): 330.

23. Ernest Best, *1 Peter*, New Century Bible (London: Oliphants, 1971), 167.

24. Hiebert (331) says, "Whenever the New Testament refers to these officers, it consistently pictures a plurality of elders in the local church (Acts 14:23; 20:17, 28; Phil 1: 1; 1 Thess 5:12 ; Jas 5:14)."

25. The Greek is *en humin*, "in you (pl.)," translated "among you" in the NASB. The idea is that each group of elders (plural) has a flock of God that is *en humin*, "among you," "in your charge," and they are responsible for that flock.

26. In the Greek text this is a single word that appears only here in the Greek New Testament, but its meaning is undisputed.

27. Hiebert, 332.

28. Since Peter was married, he could have been an elder in the same sense that others in the New Testament church were elders. See 1 Timothy 3; Titus 1.

29. Michaels, 276.

30. The idea of "shepherding" is carried forward in the designation of God's people as a "flock" (5:2, and again in 5:3). The text says the elders are to "*poimanete to ... poimnion*," an expression closely paralleled in English in the expression "shepherding the sheep." It is emphasized again when Christ is described as the "chief Shepherd" (5:4, *archipoimenos*), suggesting that elders are "under-shepherds."

31. NRSV; RSV omits the phrase from the text, putting it in a footnote. UBS³ includes the questionable word, *episkopountes*, as a class C variant ("there is a considerable degree of doubt whether the text or the apparatus contains the superior reading") in the text, but puts it in brackets. Metzger (695, 696) notes that there were good arguments for both including the disputed word and for leaving it out. But says that the committee "in order to represent the balance of external evidence and of transcriptional probabilities" decided to include the word, "but to enclose it within square brackets to indicate a certain doubt that it belongs in the text."

32. In the New Testament the terms elders, pastors, and bishops all are used for the same men or work or "office." See Wayne A. Grudem, *The First Epistle of Peter*, The Tyndale New Testament Commentaries (Grand Rapids, MI: InterVarsity Press, 1988), 187.

33. I. Howard Marshall, *1 Peter*, The IVP New Testament Commentary Series (Downers Grover, IL: InterVarsity Press, 1991), 162.

34. Cited in Wayne A. Grudem, *The First Epistle of Peter* (Grand Rapids, MI: InterVarsity Press, 1988), 187, 188.

35. Some may have been reluctant to serve because when the church was being persecuted it was dangerous to be a leader. Francis Wright Beare, *The First Epistle of Peter: The Greek Text with Introduction and Notes*, 3rd ed. (Oxford: Basil Blackwell, 1970), 199; see also Best, 169, 170.

36. Marshall, 163.

37. Hiebert, 336.

38. See 1 Timothy 5:17, 18. The prohibition is on working for "shameful gain," and would not rule out the possibility that they could still be paid. Hiebert, 336.

39. Best, 170.

40. Hiebert, 337.

41. Davids, 180.

42. Although the phrase undoubtedly remains a part of the series (it includes the same connectives, *me* or *mede* and *alla*), it is probably climactic because (1) it is third in a series of three, (2) it is longer, and (3) its major components are different grammatically—participles rather than adverb.

43. Grudem, 189. See also Hiebert, 337.

44. See Davids, 181.

45. See Hiebert, 331.

46. In rhetoric, this is known as "ethical proof" or as "ethical appeal." *"Ethos"* is the proof that is derived from the person of the speaker.

47. See: Edward Gordon Selwyn, *First Epistle of St. Peter* (New York: Macmillan and Co., 1946, 1947, 1955), 228; Hiebert, 332.

48. Some commentators take this to be Peter's way of subtly asserting his authority. It is more likely that he speaks of himself in this way to identify himself, not only with Christ, but also with his readers, who themselves share Christ's sufferings (4:13). See Michaels, 280, 281.

49. "The crown is a metaphor for the glory that the church leaders will share with Christ." Marshall, 164. It will be given at the second coming of Christ. Hiebert, 338.

50. Gk. *homoios*. Michaels (288) translates "likewise" as

"in turn," "you in turn who are younger must defer to the authority of elders," saying that *homoios* can have a reciprocal meaning, as in 3:7. See also Grudem, 191, 192.

51. UBS[3] (with NEB and JB) begins a new paragraph with 5:5, but RSV (with NRSV and NIV) makes 5:5 a part of the paragraph that includes 5:1–4. The paragraphing relates to the meaning of "younger" and "elders" in 5:5. Those who detach 5:5 from 5:1–4 probably have decided the "elders" in that verse are not the exact equivalent of the "elders" in 5:1.

52. Some believe that 5:5 refers merely to older men (see Selwyn, 227, 233); others believe it refers to the "office of an elder" (see Grudem, 192).

53. John H. Elliot, "Ministry and Church Order in the NT: A Traditio-Historical Analysis," *The Catholic Biblical Quarterly* 32 (1972): 390.

54. Michaels, 289.

55. This is the view of Davids (183, 184). Anyone under thirty might be included in the category of "more youthful."

56. To "be submissive" is a thought found frequently in the epistle in connection with the Christian's relationships: see 2:13; 2:18; 3:1, 5, 6.

57. "The image is that of a garment being tied on, and very possibly reflects John 13 where Christ, about to wash the feet of his disciples, ties on a towel to perform this humble duty." Best, 172. Harris suggests the possibility that Peter is speaking of "the symbolic dress of a religious man." Rendel Harris, "The Religious Meaning of 1 Peter V. 5," *Expositor*, series 8, vol. 18 (1919): 139.

58. Is it possible for one to lead, but still to be humble and to serve? The elders in Peter's day had Jesus's own example to prove that it could be done, in the washing of the apostles' feet (John 13) and in His death (Phil 2:4–9).

59. See Timothy M. Willis, "The Office of Elder in Church of Christ Publications, 1950-1980," *Christian Scholars Conference Papers*. vol. 2 (David Lipscomb University, Nashville, TN, July 20, 1991): 7–24.

60. Some cite Jack P. Lewis, who points out that the words for "authority" in the New Testament are never applied to elders. *Leadership Questions Confronting the Church* (Nashville,   TN: Christian Communications, 1985), 9–12. However, Lewis goes on to say (21) that elders are to be obeyed.

61. See, e.g., Robert R. Taylor, Jr., *The Elder and His Work* (Shreveport, LA: Lambert Book House, 1978), 126; and R. W. Grimsley, *The Church and Its Elders* (Abilene, TX: Quality Printing Company, 1964), 95–98.

62. *"presbuteros," A Greek-English Lexicon of the New Testament*, by William F. Arndt and F. Wilbur Gingrich,   4th revised and augmented edition (Chicago: The University of Chicago Press, 1952, 1957), 706, 707. Bornkamm (665) says that in 1 Peter 5 the elders "are a college entrusted with the guidance of the church." Gunther Bornkamm, *"presbus," Theological Dictionary of the New Testament* (*TDNT*), trans. and ed. Geoffrey Bromiley, vol. 6 (Grand Rapids, MI: Eerdmans, 1968), 651–683.

63. *episkopos* "relates to oversight or administration." J. Rohde, *"episkopos," Exegetical Dictionary of the New Testament*, eds. Horst Balz and Gerhard Schneider (Grand

Rapids, MI: Eerdmans, 1981, Eng. trans. 1991), 36. It "always connotes administrative responsibility." Selwyn, 230.

64. Ancient kings were known as shepherds; Yahweh is frequently pictured as a shepherd in the Old Testament; the future Messianic king is called a shepherd; "shepherds" was also used in the Old Testament of political and military leaders; and in the New Testament Jesus is frequently spoken of as a shepherd. J. Jeremias, "*poimen*," *TDNT*, 6:485–502.

65. For an extended discussion of the Greek words used for elders, see Lewis,13–35.

66. See: Hiebert, 337; Bornkamm *TDNT*, 6:665.

67. Lewis (34) notes that the New Testament instructions concerning elders results in a paradox: the elder should not conceive of his work in terms of authority, but the congregation should "relate to him as God's steward," and may need to be reminded to "be subject to such men."

68. Notice the distinction in this paper between "what" the elders are to do and "how" they are to do it.

WORKS CITED

Aland, Kurt, Matthew Black, Carlo M. Martini, and Allen Wikgren, eds. *The Greek New Testament*. 3rd ed. New York: United Bible Societies, 1975.

Arndt, William F., and F. Wilbur Gingrich. *A Greek-English Lexicon of the New Testament*. 4th rev. and augmented ed. Chicago: The University of Chicago Press, 1952, 1957.

Balz, Horst, and Gerhard Schneidern, eds. *Exegetical Dictionary of the New Testament.* Grand Rapids, MI: Eerdmans, 1981, Eng. trans. 1991. s.v. *"episkcmos."* by J. Rohda.

Beare, Francis Wright. *The First Epistle of Peter: The Greek Text with Introduction and Notes.* 3rd ed. Oxford: Basil Blackwell, 1970.

Best, Ernest. *1 Peter.* New Century Bible. London: Oliphants, 1971.

Black, Allen. Lecture on introduction to 1 Peter, in New Testament Exegesis, from class notes taken by Coy Roper. Harding University Graduate School of Religion, Memphis, TN, Summer, 1993.

Blum, Edwin A. "1 Peter." *The Expositor's Bible Commentary,* ed. Frank E. Gaebelein, 12 vols. Grand Rapids, MI: Zondervan, 1981.

Bromiley, Geoffrey W., ed. *The International Standard Bible Encyclopedia.* Grand Rapids, MI: Eerdmans, 1986. s.v. "Peter, First Epistle of." by R. P. Martin.

_____, ed. *Theological Dictionary of the New Testament.* Grand Rapids, MI: Eerdmans, 1968. s.v. *"presbus."* by Gunther Bornkamm; *"poimen."* by J. Jeremias.

Buttrick, George Arthur, ed. *The Interpreter's Dictionary of the Bible.* Nashville: Abingdon, 1962. s.v., "Peter, First Letter of," by W. C. van Unnik.

Carson, D. A., Douglas J. Moo, and Leon Morris. *An Introduction to the New Testament.* Grand Rapids, MI: Zondervan, 1992.

Davids, Peter H. *The First Epistle of Peter.* The New International Commentary on the New Testament. Grand Rapids, MI: Eerdmans, 1990.

Elliot, John H. *A Home for the Homeless.* Philadelphia: Fortress Press: 1981.

_____. "Ministry and Church Order in the New Testament: A Traditio-Historical Analysis." *The Catholic Biblical Quarterly* 32 (1972): 367–391.

Freedman, David Noel, ed. *The Anchor Bible Dictionary.* 6 vols. New York: Doubleday, 1992. s.v. "Peter, First Epistle of." by John H. Elliot.

Grimsley, R. W. *The Church and Its Elders.* Abilene, TX: Quality Printing Company, 1964.

Grudem, Wayne A. *The First Epistle of Peter.* The Tyndale New Testament Commentaries. Grand Rapids, MI: InterVarsity Press, 1988.

Guthrie, Donald. *New Testament Introduction.* 4th ed. Downers Grove, IL: InterVarsity Press, 1990.

Harris, Rendel. "The Religious Meaning of 1 Peter V. 5." *The Expositor.* series 8, vol. 18 (1919): 131–139.

Harrison, Everett F. *Introduction to the New Testament.* Rev. ed. Grand Rapids, MI: Eerdmans, 1964, 1971.

Hiebert, D. Edmond. "Counsel for Christ's Under-Shepherds: An Exposition of 1 Peter 5:1–4." *Bibliotheca Sacra.* 139 (1982): 330–341.

Lewis, Jack P. *Leadership Questions Confronting the Church.* Nashville, TN: Christian Communications, 1985.

Marshall, I. Howard. *1 Peter.* The IVP New Testament Commentary. Downers Grover, IL: InterVarsity Press, 1991.

Metzger, Bruce M. *A Textual Commentary on the Greek New Testament.* New York: United Bible Societies, 1971.

Michaels, J. Ramsey. *1 Peter.* Word Biblical Commentary 49. Waco, TX: Word Books, 1988.

Mills, Watson E., ed. *Mercer Dictionary of the Bible.* Macon, GA: Mercer University Press, 1990. s.v. "Peter, Letters of." by Richard A. Spencer.

Perrin, Norman, and Dennis C. Duling. *The New Testament: An Introduction.* 2nd ed. New York: Harcourt Brace Jovanovich, 1974, 1982.

Selwyn, Edward Gordon. *First Epistle of St. Peter.* New York: Macmillan and Co., 1955.

Talbert, Charles H. "Once Again: The Plan of 1 Peter." Pages 141–151 in *Perspectives on First Peter.* Edited by Charles H. Talbert. Macon, GA: Mercer University Press, 1986.

Taylor, Robert R., Jr. *The Elder and His Work.* Shreveport, LA: Lambert Book House, 1978.

Tenney, Merrill C. *The New Testament: An Historical and Analytic Survey.* Grand Rapids, MI: Eerdmans, 1955.

Willis, Timothy M. "The Office of Elder in Church of Christ Publications, 1950-1980." *Christian Scholars Conference Papers*, vol. 2. David Lipscomb University, Nashville, TN, July 20, 1991.

Young's Analytical Concordance to the Bible. 22nd American ed., rev. Grand Rapids, MI: Eerdmans, n.d.

4

WOMEN IN THE LINEAGE OF THE MESSIAH

AUTUMN S. RICHARDSON

Chances are you have a few "nuts" on your family tree. A limb or two you sometimes wish no one knew about? I do. We all do. Family is messy, complicated, and sometimes downright embarrassing or painful to talk about. We all have disappointments, tragedies, and even scandals that happen within our families. Baggage. When asked about my family, I mostly stick to telling about the members I'm close to, the ones not living in sin, the ones I'm most proud to call mine. Why do we do that? Probably because we don't want to feel ashamed or embarrassed. Because we don't want people to think there might be something in our DNA that could cause us to act, look, or be like the less-than-savory characters we are kin to.

When the Holy Spirit tells us about Jesus's earthly family tree, though, He doesn't shy away from the scandalous or the embarrassing. In fact, He highlights it in the women He chooses to mention in Matthew's genealogy of

Christ. In this Gospel, written to the Jews so they would believe Jesus was indeed the Messiah, I probably would have chosen to mention matriarchs such as Sarah, Rebekah, or Rachel. Included instead are five shady, disreputable, less than fortunate women. Since this was a time when Jews only traced their lineages through the men, choosing to include these women seems a bold, intentional statement on God's part.

The first woman mentioned in Matthew's account of Jesus's lineage is Tamar (Matt 1:3). There are three Tamars in Scripture. This is the one we often skip over in Bible class. The one who posed as a prostitute to trick her father-in-law Judah into sleeping with her (Gen 38).

Next is Rahab, the actual prostitute—a Gentile Canaanite woman who made a career out of sin (Matt 1:5; Josh 2).

Ruth, also a Gentile mentioned in verse 5, was a widow converted from paganism to serve Yahweh and to care for her mother-in-law Naomi after both suffered a great loss. She became a part of Jesus's family tree when she married Boaz (Ruth 4).

The fourth woman mentioned is Bathsheba (Matt 1:6), a young woman caught in adultery with King David, who killed her Hittite husband (2 Sam 11). In fact, instead of being called by name, she is referred to in the genealogy as Uriah's wife. Whether she was a willing participant in the affair is not clear, but her reputation would have been one of scandal either way.

Finally, we have Mary (Matt 1:16), an unwed teenage mother. We know she was a virgin because scripture tells us so, but who would have believed that at the time (Luke 1:27)?

Why? Why did God in his infinite wisdom think this was a good idea? Why remind the Jews of these painful moments in their history? Why announce the coming King of Glory with less than glorious stories? The Jews knew the Messiah was coming through the lineage of Judah and David, so they knew these women were part of the story, but why dredge up the ugly past? These were not their finest moments.

Maybe it's because these women were unlikely and unsung heroes in the story of the Jews. Tamar secured her and her family's future, despite Judah's efforts to abandon her, and was considered "more righteous" than him. (Gen 38:26). Rahab displayed courage and faith in hiding the spies and trusting that she and her family would be saved as a result (Josh 2). She then marries into the Jewish nation and becomes the mother of Boaz. Ruth, a Gentile, had an opportunity to start a new life after her husband died but chose instead to serve and care for her mother-in-law and follow Naomi's God, Yahweh (Ruth 1:16). She is then redeemed and loved by Rahab's son, Boaz. Bathsheba committed adultery with David and suffered great loss in her life but raised the great king Solomon and made sure he followed David on the throne of Israel (1 Kgs 1). Then, we are introduced to Mary, a virgin who would bear the son of God (Matt 1).

Maybe God wanted to foreshadow or emphasize what the coming Messiah would bring with Him: inclusion of the Gentiles, love for the outcasts, salvation to the sinful, grace to the least deserving. He'd done those things already in these women's lives, but it was about to happen on a worldwide scale.

Maybe they were included so we could see that despite Jesus having a lot of baggage in his family, he remained sinless. Sometimes we like to blame pedigree for the way we turned out, but Jesus shows us DNA doesn't determine our destiny.

Whatever the reason God chose to include these women in the lineage of Christ, we should take note and take comfort. Jesus came to the world through imperfect, disgraceful characters in order to save me, an imperfect woman in need of His grace. Thanks be to God for that grace (2 Cor 9:14–15) and for using these women according to His purpose (Rom 8:28)!

5

LED BY THE SPIRIT

THOMAS TIDWELL

This is a difficult topic.

In Christendom, especially in the denominational world, there is a great deal of misunderstanding concerning the Holy Spirit and how He works in revealing the truth. Even in the Lord's church, the work of the Holy Spirit, (especially *how* the Spirit works), is discussed and debated, as some Christians struggle to understand the Spirit. We seem (?) to have a good grasp on what God the Father does (but do we really?), and what the Son did (and continues to do); but when it comes to the Holy Spirit, we are not sure, mainly because of the diversity of opinions in and out of the church.

These misunderstandings have and will continue to influence the church in many ways. For example, many claim to be led by the Spirit and claim that the Holy Spirit guides them by their feelings, emotions, and thoughts. Often these feelings and emotions are in direct contradiction to the inspired word of God. It is not about the will of God, or even trying to ascertain the will of God—it is all about "being led by emotions and feelings" that many believe are given by the Spirit, and these "leadings" tell them what God wants and desires in their lives. Often these "leadings" are in direct contradiction to the Word of God.

This is an important topic, and we need to make sure that we understand what God's word says about the Spirit. We need to understand the work He did in the first century and what He does today through and by means of the Word.

As a young man, my mother took me to a "holiness church." I do not remember hearing a lot of Scripture (or I may not have paid much attention). I remember a man who "became a Christian" who "prayed through" on the mourner's bench for a period of two to three days until he "prayed through and was saved." The emphasis for this young man, and most in this church, was the feelings he was experiencing at that time, and he judged his salvation, not on what the Bible clearly taught, but on emotions that come and go.

Feelings and emotions are not always good guides. Sometimes we may feel ill or may be depressed due to sickness. We may be joyful over a new child born, a better job offer, or a new challenge, and believe that the Holy Spirit has worked in our lives in a "powerful way." We know that joy is a manifestation of the fruit of the Spirit (Gal 5:22), and hence, in the minds of some, is a manifestation of being in a right relationship with God. However, when some do not "feel joy" or happiness, some think that the Holy Spirit has "left" the Christian, and feelings of guilt overwhelm them. They think they can never be the Christian that they need to be, and, often, they give up. (I know this from personal experience—I kept wondering if the Holy Spirit was in my life or not, based on my feelings, a "throwback" to the church in which I was reared.)

The topic of the Holy Spirit is one that needs further study, so that we may be able to ". . . give an answer to every man a reason for the hope that is in us" (1 Pet 3:15).

Jack Exum, in a short book titled, *The Holy Spirit*, warned of a further danger when he wrote,

> The Holy Spirit is Sovereign Deity. He does not have to report to you and me concerning his activities and because He expresses himself in different ways at different times, should only prove the point. *You cannot put the Holy Spirit into a box. You cannot lock him in the limits of your own mind.* This bothers us! Primarily because some make claims that the inspired word of the Spirit would not endorse, we tend to go to the opposite extreme. We want to tame the Spirit, limit the Spirit's activities, deny the Spirit's providence, and work. Both extremes should be avoided.[1]

MIRACULOUS MANIFESTATIONS TODAY?

Many today claim that they have the miraculous manifestations of the Holy Spirit that were in fulfillment of promises made by Jesus *specifically* to the apostles in the first century. Jesus in John 13–16 emphasizes the work of the Spirit and how the Spirit would reveal the truth. He made the apostles some promises concerning the Spirit that were specific to them. Notice these passages and the *context*, which helps us to see to whom the promises were made.

In John 13 Jesus washed the disciples' feet and emphasized that the disciples must become as the teacher. He taught them to love one another—not just "feel it in their heart" but to act on it by their deeds. He had exemplified that to the disciples, and we must follow in His steps as well.

Jesus then predicted His betrayal by Judas. Jesus knew (and still knows) people's hearts and sin and warned Judas —but Judas did not listen or heed the warning. Do we? (John 13:27–30).

He stressed the importance of love among the disciples. They would have to set the example as He did while He was on earth, and the greatest example is found in the cross. He tells them to "Love one another as I have loved you." (John 13:34). He set the example of being there, teaching them what God wanted them to know, and loving them, as exemplified on the cross. Beloved, we must challenge one another in our growth for God! We must lovingly rebuke when others get "wrong-headed" notions yet listen when are rebuked for "wrong-headed" notions of our own.

He stressed to them that He wanted them to be with Him. He wants the same for us today.

He stressed that "If we see Him (Jesus), we see the

Father." Hence, the more we are like Jesus, the more we see the Father and His love for humanity! How else can we know Jesus other than through the Word the Holy Spirit inspired?

Jesus would give them (context still refers specifically to the eleven disciples, as Judas was not there) the Spirit as the Helper in John 14:15–18. Notice that Jesus said concerning the Spirit, "whom the world cannot receive, because it neither sees him nor knows him." Yet they (the disciples/later apostles) would know Him for He dwelled in them and would be with them.

The Spirit would "teach them all things and bring all things to their remembrance" (John 14:26).

In John 15:26 Jesus stated that He would send the Holy Spirit from the Father (this would happen after His ascension to heaven—see Acts 1–2).

The Spirit's work would be through the apostles as they preached the gospel to the world, and would ". . . convict the world of sin, righteousness and judgment." (John 16:8–15). The conviction of the world of sin would come as the gospel was preached. In John 16:13 Jesus told the apostles that the Spirit ". . .will guide you into all truth." There would be no need for further revelation other than the Bible, God's word. Hence, if we want to know God's will; if we will be "led by the Spirit," we must study inspired Scripture to show ourselves approved unto God. Most importantly, we should live by Scripture teaching, and when we find that we are not in accordance with God's will, we must repent.

HOW ARE CHRISTIANS TODAY LED BY THE SPIRIT?

From the above passages, we know that we are led by the Spirit today through, or by means of, the word of God.

How are we led by the Holy Spirit? Christians are led by the Spirit. In Romans 8:12–17 Scriptures teach

> So then, brothers, we are debtors, not to the flesh, to live according to the flesh. For if you live according to the flesh you will die, but *if by the Spirit you put to death the deeds of the body*, you will live. For all *who are led by the Spirit of God are sons of God*. For you did not receive the spirit of slavery to fall back into fear, but you have received the Spirit of adoption as sons, by whom we cry, "Abba! Father!" *The Spirit himself bears witness with our spirit that we are children of God, and if children*, then heirs —heirs of God and fellow heirs with Christ, provided we suffer with him in order that we may also be glorified with him.

The above passage makes these things clear:

1. When we live by the teachings of the Spirit, then we will put to death the deeds of the body.
2. All who are led by the Spirit are the sons of God.

Sometimes we struggle with this because we hope the Spirit will keep us from sin and transgressions of God's law. The fact is, however, that we choose to listen to the message of the Spirit (via the Word of God).

The above shows that when we study Scripture; when we have open hearts and minds to the word of God, and, more importantly, *live that word*, we are being led by the Spirit. We must understand that Jesus promised the Spirit in a miraculous way to the apostles, and in a time when God's revelation was not complete, they would be led by the Spirit. Today, God has given us the completed revelation—the Word of God, and we judge right and wrong, good and evil, by the written, Holy Spirit-inspired word of God. Hence the importance in spending time in the written word of God.

We can then see the *vital* importance of spending time in meditating on God's word. Let us allow ourselves to be taught by the Spirit of God in His word!

Let us notice how the Spirit used Scripture to teach about Himself and His work in two different letters to two different churches.

As Paul dealt with the problems in the Galatian church notice how he continually emphasized the gospel and the need to know and *live* the gospel.

There were some in the Galatian church that were teaching and/or being taught that they had to keep the law (in this context it would have reference to keeping the Law of Moses), which had been done away with on the cross. Many of the "newer converts" to Christ, having come from Judaism, would have continued to keep the Law of Moses, which was done away with at the cross. The Jewish Christian would have tried to bind Mosaic law-keeping upon the new Christians, Jews, or Gentiles. Paul corrects this falsehood by pointing out that they received the Spirit by the hearing of faith (Gal 3:2). He goes on to argue that

> "If you have begun in the Spirit, are you now perfected in the flesh?" Paul asked if, "Does he who supplies the Spirit to you and works miracles among you do so by works of the law, or by *hearing with faith*— just as Abraham "believed God, and it was counted to him as righteousness"?"

Jesus came to fulfill the law as he clearly stated in Matthew 5:17–18. Once it was fulfilled, then it was done away with.

In Galatians 5:16 Paul pointed out that if they "Walk by the Spirit then they will not fulfill the lust of the flesh."

WALKING BY THE SPIRIT IS WALKING BY THE GOSPEL

Notice these further passages from the book of Galatians and Romans . . .

> But the law is not of faith, rather "The one who does them shall live by them." Christ redeemed us from the curse of the law by becoming a curse for us—for it is written, "Cursed is everyone who is hanged on a tree"— so that in Christ Jesus the blessing of Abraham might

come to the Gentiles, so that we might receive the promised Spirit through faith (Gal 3:12–14).

You are severed from Christ, you who would be justified by the law; you have fallen away from grace. For through the Spirit, by faith, we ourselves eagerly wait for the hope of righteousness. For in Christ Jesus neither circumcision nor uncircumcision counts for anything, but only faith working through love. You who would be justified by the law, you are fallen away from grace. We eagerly wait for the hope of righteousness (Gal 5:4–6).

You are severed from Christ, you who would be justified by the law; you have fallen away from grace. For through the Spirit, by faith, we ourselves eagerly wait for the hope of righteousness. For in Christ Jesus neither circumcision nor uncircumcision counts for anything, but only faith working through love (Gal 5:16–18).

In Galatians 5:19–24 Paul contrasts the works of the flesh in verses 19–21 with the fruits of the Spirit in Galatians 5:22–23. Why is there a difference? The works of the flesh lead to selfish acts without regards to anyone else. The fruits of the Spirit, applied in our lives, will show Jesus to those around us. But the fruit of the Spirit is love, joy, peace . . .

If we live by the Spirit, by the Spirit let us also walk (Gal 5:25).

Romans 1:16 "The gospel is God's power unto salvation to everyone that believes." (Not the law — by the law, no one could be justified (see also Rom 3:20).

Sin shall not have dominion over you, for you are not under the law but under grace (Rom 6:14).

Romans 8:1 "There is therefore now no condemnation to them that are in Christ Jesus who walk not after the flesh but after the Spirit"—What does this mean to walk after the Spirit?

For the law of the Spirit of life has made me free from the law of sin and death (Rom 8:2).

For God has done what the law, weakened by the flesh, could not do. By sending his own Son in the likeness of sinful flesh and for sin, he condemned sin in the flesh In order that the righteous requirement of the law might be fulfilled in us, who walk not according to the flesh but according to the Spirit. For those who live according to the flesh set their minds on the things of the flesh, *but those who live according to the Spirit set their minds on the things of the Spirit. For to set the mind on the flesh is death, but to set the mind on the Spirit is life and peace.* For the mind that is set on the flesh is hostile to God, for it does not submit to God's law; indeed, it cannot. Those who are in the flesh cannot please God Those who are in the flesh cannot please God. *You, however, are not in the flesh but in the Spirit, if in fact the Spirit of God dwells in you.*

Anyone who does not have the Spirit of Christ does not belong to him. But if Christ is in you, although the body is dead because of sin, the Spirit is life because of righteousness. If the Spirit of him who raised Jesus from the dead dwells in you, he who raised Christ Jesus from the dead will also give life to your mortal bodies through his Spirit who dwells in you (Rom 8:3–11) [emphasis mine].

So then, brothers, we are debtors, not to the flesh, to live according to the flesh. *For if you live according to the flesh you will die*, but if by the Spirit you put to death the deeds of the body, you will live. *For all who are led by the Spirit of God are sons of God.* For you did not receive the spirit of slavery to fall back into fear, but you have received the Spirit of adoption as sons, by whom we cry, "Abba! Father!" The Spirit himself bears witness with our spirit that we are children of God, and if children, then heirs— heirs of God and fellow heirs with Christ, provided we suffer with him in order that we may also be glorified with him (Rom 8:12–17).

Do you not know that your bodies are members of Christ? Shall I then take the members of Christ and make them members of a prostitute? Never! Or do you not know that he who is joined to a prostitute becomes one body with her? For, as it is written, "The two will become one flesh." But he who is joined to the Lord becomes one spirit with him. Flee from sexual immorality. Every other sin a person commits is outside the body, but the sexually immoral person sins against his own body. *Or do you not know that your body is a temple of the Holy Spirit within you, whom you have from God?* You are not your own, for you were bought with a price. So glorify God in your body (1 Cor 6:15–20).

For this reason I bow my knees before the Father, from whom every family in heaven and on earth is named, *that according to the riches of his glory he may grant you to be strengthened with power through his Spirit in your inner being, so that Christ may dwell in your hearts through faith—* (result) that you, being rooted and grounded in love, may have strength to comprehend with all the saints what is the breadth and length and height and depth, and to know the love of Christ that surpasses knowledge, that you may be filled with all the fullness of God (Eph 3:14–19).

And you, who once were alienated and hostile in mind, doing evil deeds, he has now reconciled in his body of flesh by his death, in order to present you holy and blameless and above reproach before him, *if indeed you continue in the faith, stable and steadfast, not shifting from the hope of the gospel that you heard, which has been proclaimed in all creation under heaven,* and of which I, Paul, became a minister (Col 1:21–23).

There is much ado made about the indwelling of the Holy Spirit. We need to rid ourselves of our preconceived notions and allow the Scriptures to speak on this matter. When allowing Scripture to speak (2 Tim 3:16) we can then make an honest evaluation about the work of the Holy Spirit dwelling in the Christian. When we allow Scripture to speak, then we will add the fruit of the Spirit in our lives—love, joy, peace, longsuffering, kindness, goodness, faithfulness, gentleness, self-control. Against such there is no law. The scriptures argue that they can make the person of God complete and equipped for every good work. But what is the indwelling of the Holy Spirit? The indwelling is commonly explained to be the inner promptings of the Holy Spirit. We are told that we need to listen to God speaking to us through the Holy Spirit who will help us and tell us what we should do. Is this correct? Would we listen if He spoke to us? Did the world in Jesus's time listen to Jesus? Some did, others didn't. Will we listen to the "inspired by the Spirit" Word of God, or to man as to the most important matters regarding salvation?

To summarize, we need to listen to the Word of God and be led by the Spirit in what we know to be the truth!

Who or what controls your life?

ENDNOTES

Jack Exum, *The Holy Spirit: How He Works in the Life of the Christian Today*. (Life Spring Resources, Franklin Springs, GA. No Copyright): 2–13.

6
THE QUIET WOMEN IN ACTS

DIANNE TAYS

I n his instructions to wives in 1 Peter 3:3–4, Peter says that a woman's beauty shouldn't come from the outside, with jewelry and clothes, but

> it should be that of your inner self, the unfading beauty of a gentle and quiet spirit, which is of great worth in God's sight. For this is the way the holy women of the past who put their hope in God used to make themselves beautiful.

What does it mean to have a gentle and quiet spirit? Gentle can mean kind or amiable. It can also mean soft or delicate.[1] We could substitute these words in place of gentle in 1 Peter 3 to say inner beauty is being kind, being amiable. Our inner beauty should be soft and delicate like a flower. Quiet can mean gentle, easy going, still, free from noise or uproar.[2] If we put these words together to describe someone with a gentle and quiet spirit, we would say they are kind, amiable, soft, delicate, gentle, easygoing, and free from uproar. In the book of Acts, we meet several women who are examples of this type of inner beauty. These women used their talents to tell others about Jesus and to help spread the Good News to all the world.

First, in Acts 9:36–40, we meet a woman named Dorcas. We learn from verse 37 that Dorcas had become ill and died. At that same time, Peter was in the city of Lydda, which according to verse 38, was near the city of Joppa where Dorcas lived. The disciples in Joppa sent two men for Peter. When Peter arrived in Joppa, he was taken to the upstairs room where the body of Dorcas had been placed. Dorcas, also called Tabitha, was an important member of the church in Joppa. The description we have of Dorcas is that she was "always doing good and helping the poor" (vs. 36). We know from verse 39 that Dorcas also made clothing for lots of the widows. These women were in the house crying and showing the clothes to Peter. Peter prayed to the Lord and was able to raise Dorcas from the dead. Because of this miracle, many people believed and were brought to Christ. Dorcas saw a need among the widows and poor of her community and used her talents to fill that need. We should all use the talents we have to further the Lord's church. When we use our talents to help others, we will be showing them Christ living in us. We will be letting our light shine in a dark world.

In Acts 16, we meet two more Christian women. When Paul arrived at Lystra, he met a young man named Timothy. We learn from verse 1 that Timothy's mother, Eunice, was a Christian. 2 Timothy 1:5 tells us that Timothy had a "sincere faith, which first lived in your grandmother Lois and in your mother Eunice." These two women had passed their faith down to Timothy. They had followed the Lord's instruction to "train a child in the way he should go" (Prov 22:6). Their teachings to Timothy had led him to be a Christian. Acts 16:2 tells us that Timothy was well spoken of by the believers at Lystra. Later, Timothy became a traveling companion to Paul. From Paul's letters to Timothy, we know that Timothy remained faithful. Because of the influence of his mother and grandmother, Timothy became a worker for the Lord and influenced others to follow Christ. We should all be Christian examples to our families and influence them to put Christ first in their lives. As Proverbs 22:6 continues, then "when he is old, he will not turn from it." Our influence can continue for generations.

Another gentle and quiet spirit we meet in Acts is Lydia. In Acts 16:13–14, we learn that Paul had made his way to the city of Philippi, a Roman colony (verse 12). Usually, when Paul entered a city, he would go first to the synagogue. The fact that Paul did not go to a synagogue probably meant that Philippi did not have a local synagogue.[3] According to verse 13, on the Sabbath Paul and his companions went to the river looking for a place to pray. A group of women was meeting at the river. Paul and his group sat down and began talking to the women. In the group was a woman from the city of Thyatira named Lydia. In Acts 16:14, we find that Lydia was a business owner. She was a seller of purple cloth. We also learn that she was a worshiper of God. According to verse 14, the Lord opened her heart to respond to Paul's message. Lydia and the members of her household were baptized. Afterward, she invited Paul and his group into her home. In Acts 16, Paul and Silas are thrown in prison for teaching about Christ. In verse 40, we learn that when Paul and Silas were released from prison, they went to Lydia's house. Lydia, a new Christian, was already serving the Lord. She had opened her home for other brothers and sisters to meet. Paul and Silas went to her home to encourage them. We should be willing to open our homes to other people and use our homes to teach others about Christ.

The last woman from Acts that we will look at is Priscilla. We are introduced to Priscilla in Acts 18. Priscilla was the wife of Aquila. Priscilla and Aquila worked together as tentmakers. Priscilla also worked with Aquila in teaching others. Paul had left Priscilla and Aquila in Ephesus. According to Acts 18:24, a man named Apollos had come to Ephesus. "He was a learned man, with a thorough knowledge of the Scriptures." Apollos only knew about the baptism of John. Aquila and Priscilla invited Apollos to their home and according to Acts 18:26 taught him "more adequately." In Romans 16 and 1 Corinthians 16, we read that Priscilla and Aquila opened their home to Christians as a meeting place for worship. Priscilla worked beside her husband to help further the growth of the church. We should reach out to teach others about Christ. We can teach a children's class, a ladies' class, or just teach those we are in contact with every day by showing them Christ living in us.

There are other women mentioned in Acts who worked for the Lord about whom we don't have as much information. In Acts 12 we read that Peter, after being released from prison, went to the house of Mary, the mother of John Mark. Acts 12:12 states that "many people had gathered and were praying" for Peter at Mary's house. Mary had opened her home to other Christians for a prayer meeting. Another believer mentioned in the house is Rhoda, a servant girl. When Peter knocked on the door at Mary's house, Rhoda answered the door. Verse 14 tells us that she was "overjoyed" to hear Peter's voice. By opening her home to others, Mary was able to influence her son, other Christians, and her servant, Rhoda.

In Acts 17:12, we learn there were also several prominent Greek women who believed in Christ in the city of Berea. Acts 17:34 tells us of a believer named Damaris. In Acts 21, when Paul was leaving Tyre to head to Jerusalem, we read that all the disciples there, "including wives and children" (verse 5) went with him out of the city. They all prayed with Paul on the beach before he departed. Women everywhere can serve Christ in whatever situation they find themselves. Every congregation has women who quietly serve in the background visiting the sick, sending cards, preparing meals, praying with other women, preparing communion, teaching classes, and opening their home to others.

Several verses in the Bible instruct all Christians to have a spirit that is gentle and quiet. Colossians 3:12 states

"Therefore, as God's chosen people, holy and dearly loved, clothe yourselves with compassion, kindness, humility, gentleness and patience." Galatians 5:22 tells us that "the fruit of the Spirit is love, joy, peace, patience, kindness, goodness, faithfulness." In 1 Timothy 2:2 we are told to pray and be thankful "for kings and all those in authority, that we may live peaceful and quiet lives in all godliness and holiness." Proverbs 15:1 reminds us that "a gentle answer turns away wrath." 1 Peter 3:15 tells us to "always be prepared to give an answer to everyone who asks you to give the reason for the hope that you have." This verse goes on to say to give our answer "with gentleness and respect." As we teach other people, we need to always remember to treat them with gentleness and respect. We need to think about how we say something as well as the words we use. We need to let others see Christ in us and our words.

Most of all, we should follow the example that our Lord set for us. In Matthew 11:29–30, Jesus says "Take my yoke upon you and learn from me, for I am gentle and humble in heart, and you will find rest for your souls." In 2 Corinthians 10:1 Paul describes Christ by saying "By the meekness and gentleness of Christ, I appeal to you." Jesus showed his gentle and quiet spirit in Mark 10:16 when he took children in his arms and blessed them, in John 13:5 when he washed the feet of the disciples, and in John 8 when he dealt with the adulterous woman. He was gentle with Peter when Peter was trying to walk on water and took his eyes off Jesus. The word gentle was also used to describe God in 1 Kings 19. Elijah was afraid and had hidden in a cave. The Lord told him to go stand on the mountain and wait for the Lord to pass by. In verses 11–12 we are told that the Lord was not in the wind, not in the earthquake, and not in the fire, but that he passed as a "gentle whisper." Ephesians 4:2 teaches us to "Be completely humble and gentle; be patient, bearing with one another in love." In Philippians 4:5 we are told to "Let your gentleness be evident to all." We should all try to have a quiet and gentle spirit when we deal with others.

An excellent example of a quiet and gentle spirit is Barbara Dillon. My husband, Mike, and I first met Barbara at the Christian Student Center on the campus of the University of North Alabama. We were both students at UNA and spent a lot of our time at the Christian Student Center. Fred Dillon was the director of the Christian Student Center. We became friends with Brother Dillon's son Kevin and met Barbara when she and Kevin married.

Barbara and Kevin have been involved in Christian service all their lives. They both had parents whose lives were dedicated to serving the Lord and they were taught to serve the Lord. Over the years, Kevin and Barbara have worked with several of our local congregations. Barbara has always been right there supporting Kevin in his work. Kevin ministers to residents in assisted living and nursing homes. Barbara is there supporting this work also.

Barbara has also spent many years working for and supporting Heritage Christian University. In her early years of working at Heritage (then International Bible College), Barbara worked in the nursery that International

Bible College provided for the families enrolled as students. She loved working with the children. She still talks about some of the children she knew and always loves visiting with their families when they come back to visit the university.

Barbara has a son Richard and daughter-in-law Jessica. Richard is continuing the family tradition of working for the Lord's church. Barbara loves her family and is very proud of them. She especially loves her grandson, Elijah. Barbara is an example of the mother and grandmother mentioned in Acts 16. She has passed down to her child and grandchild her sincere faith and love for Christ.

Most importantly, Barbara's love for the Lord and His church is very evident every day. She loves to sing songs of praise, study God's word, and worship the Lord. The words kind, soft, and gentle describe Barbara Dillon.

ENDNOTES

[1.] *Webster's Ninth New Collegiate Dictionary.* (Springfield, MA: Merriam-Webster, 1987), 511.

[2.] *Webster's Ninth New Collegiate Dictionary.* 967.

[3.] *Holman Illustrated Bible Dictionary.* (Nashville, TN: Holman Bible Publishers, 2003), 1289.

BIBLIOGRAPHY

Holman Illustrated Bible Dictionary. Nashville, TN: Holman Bible Publishers, 2003.

The NIV Study Bible. Red Letter Edition. Grand Rapids, MI: Zondervan. 1985.

Webster's Ninth New Collegiate Dictionary. Springfield, MA: Merriam-Webster, 1987.

7

THE WOMAN WITH BLOOD

MELISSA MCFERRIN

J airus was a man who demonstrated incredible trust in Jesus's willingness and ability to perform miracles. Although he was a leader of the synagogue, Jairus humbled himself, begging for Jesus to heal his ailing daughter. When she died before they reached her, Jairus still drew comfort from the encouraging words of the Lord. Because of Jairus' belief, Jesus returned his daughter to him alive and well.

In the middle of all three Gospel accounts of Jairus, there occurs another story. At first glance, it appears unrelated by any tie except timing. We will see, however, that Jairus and the woman described here shared a common faith. Let's read Mark 5:25–34[1], which takes place as Jairus and Jesus are making their way to Jairus' house:

A woman who had had a hemorrhage for twelve years, and had endured much at the hands of many physicians, and had spent all that she had and was not helped at all, but rather had grown worse—after hearing about Jesus, she came up in the crowd behind Him and touched His cloak. For she thought, "If I just touch His garments, I will get well." Immediately the flow of her blood was dried up; and she felt in her body that she was healed of her affliction. Immediately Jesus, perceiving in Himself that the power proceeding from Him had gone forth, turned around in the crowd and said, "Who touched My garments?" And His disciples said to Him, "You see the crowd pressing in on You, and You say, 'Who touched Me?'" And He looked around to see the woman who had done this. But the woman fearing and trembling, aware of what had happened to her, came and fell down before Him and told Him the whole truth. And He said to her, "Daughter, your faith has made you well; go in peace and be healed of your affliction."

Both Jairus and this woman show us examples of great faith. Let us walk through the passage, absorbing each piece of information as we build a picture of who this woman was and what happened to her.

First, she was a woman. Some women, like Lydia, were successful in business and acted as head of their households (Acts 16:14–15). Others, like Joanna the wife of Herod's steward, married influential men and supported good works with their personal wealth (Luke 8:1–3). Most women, however, depended upon others to care for them;

Paul described how the church should support widows in 1 Timothy 5:3–16. We are not told this woman's original station in life, but we know she grew impoverished seeking a cure for her illness.

Second, she had a hemorrhage. Leviticus 15:25–27 outlines the law for women with an ongoing flow of blood:

> Now if a woman has a discharge of her blood many days, not at the period of her menstrual impurity, or if she has a discharge beyond that period, all the days of her impure discharge she shall continue as though in her menstrual impurity; she is unclean. Any bed on which she lies all the days of her discharge shall be to her like her bed at menstruation; and every thing on which she sits shall be unclean, like her uncleanness at that time. Likewise, whoever touches them shall be unclean and shall wash his clothes and bathe in water and be unclean until evening.

Additionally, verse 19 tells us that whoever touched her would be unclean as well. Sometimes we get the idea that people like this woman would have been complete outcasts from society, never having any human contact or being able to participate in the activities of the community. For lepers, that was true. The law commanded that they live outside the camp. But people with other forms of uncleanness were much less limited. Obviously the woman interacted with her doctors, and she was allowed to mingle with the crowd. We have to remember that uncleanness was undesirable, yes, but it was not sinful. A person could become unclean doing any number of regular tasks, and he or she simply had to follow the process—usually offering a sacrifice and/or bathing in water and waiting until evening—to become clean again.

One major area that this woman's illness would have impacted her life, however, involved her relationship with her husband, if she was married. According to Leviticus 20:18, a couple who lay together during the wife's flow of blood was to be "cut off from among their people." Assuming the same law applies to irregular bleeding as to regular, this woman and her husband, if she had one, had to abstain from sexual intercourse for the duration of her illness.

The woman had been living with her affliction for twelve years. Can you imagine? For over a decade, she had suffered the pain and nastiness of constant bleeding. She did not have the medicine or even the hygiene products we have now to help her manage. And it was getting worse. She subjected herself to the embarrassment and discomfort of seeing many doctors and spent all her money, but to no avail. Her life was draining away with her blood.

Enter Jesus. Do not suppose that the woman thought she would try touching Him, hoping it would work, only because she had run out of other options. That is not the picture in the Bible. When she heard about Jesus, she knew, without a doubt, that He would cure her. Her faith was so sure that she did not even need to make direct contact. She snuck up, touched His garment, and was healed.

Is our faith so certain? Do we bring our troubles to Jesus without doubts or reservations? When we do, we will see Him work in big ways. First Peter 5:6–7 urges, "Therefore humble yourselves under the mighty hand of God, that He may exalt you at the proper time, casting all your anxiety on Him, because He cares for you." That describes exactly what this woman did.

The woman's experience with illness mirrors our experience with sin. Sin is a disease of the soul. Some believe that a major reason Jesus did so much physical healing while He was here was to give us a picture of the spiritual healing He offers. Jesus called Himself a physician for sinners (Mark 2:17). The woman had exhausted every available earthly cure. None worked. In the same way, the cure for sin cannot be found on earth. It is spiritual in nature, and it is found only in approaching and touching the Son of God. The shedding of His blood cleanses us from the figurative hemorrhaging of our sin.

When the woman was healed, she felt it happen. At the same time, Jesus noticed the exercise of His power. How did that work? Something similar occurred with Paul in Acts 19:11–12, where articles of clothing he had touched retained the ability to heal. With Jesus, did the healing force emanating from Him affect anyone who drew near enough to contact it? Did it require Jesus's attention, or was it automatic? We do not know. The point is that Jesus healed the woman, and they both felt it.

Our relationship with God is just as emotional as it is

mental. We should have feelings connected to our faith! In 2 Corinthians 7:11, Paul described the gamut of emotions displayed by the Corinthians in response to a situation in their fellowship: earnestness, sorrow, indignation, fear, longing, zeal. The fruit of the Spirit includes love, joy, peace, etc. (Gal 5:22–23). The fact that humans are emotional creatures is part of what marks us as being made in the image of God, who is also an emotional being. For example, the Spirit of God is grieved when we speak harsh words (Eph 4:29–31), and there is joy in heaven when a sinner repents (Luke 15:7). When we touch Jesus, we both feel it.

Back in our story, Jesus knew who had touched Him. Notice that "He looked around to see the woman who had done this" (Mark 5:32). Still, He asked the question, "Who touched my garments?" (Mark 5:30). Why? Jesus was a master at using any situation as a teaching moment. He used this opportunity to make a point to the disciples and to the woman. Recall that the woman was behind Jesus, and that she touched His cloak, not Him. He could not see her nor feel her. Yet He knew that (A) someone had touched Him, (B) that person touched His garments, and (C) it was a woman. The disciples thought it was absurd that Jesus tried to single out anyone in the midst of the pressing crowd. They missed the subtler message—that Jesus's divine knowledge extended to the details of events He had never observed.

As for the woman, Jesus was inviting her to come forward. He could have pointed her out with His eyes closed, but He let her approach Him. She responded with fear and trembling as she returned to Him and confessed everything. Why did Jesus stop in the middle of His important errand with Jairus? The woman had already been healed, and she knew it was Jesus who did it. But He could not let her leave without bringing her story to light and giving her some words of encouragement. Jesus does not want to just brush our lives. He wants to be Lord of our lives, but when we slip away, we have to come back to Him. This is the only time in Scripture Jesus fondly called a woman "Daughter." When she walked away the final time, everyone present knew of her great faith and that she was cured of her illness, able to be clean again for the first time in twelve years. She was a changed woman.

There is still much left for us to do once we have been healed by Jesus. For the woman, Leviticus 15:28–30 dictated:

> When she becomes clean from her discharge, she shall count off for herself seven days; and afterward she will be clean. Then on the eighth day she shall take for herself two turtledoves or two young pigeons and bring them in to the priest, to the doorway of the tent of meeting. The priest shall offer the one for a sin offering and the other for a burnt offering. So the priest shall make atonement on her behalf before the Lord because of her impure discharge.

The woman was physically healed, but she was not clean until she followed through with the steps described in the law. Sometimes we focus on the moment of salvation and neglect the life of faithfulness that must follow.

We are on a journey, a mission, like the woman. If we model our faith after hers, our journey will begin with Jesus saying, "Daughter, take courage; your faith has made you well; go in peace and be healed of your affliction." (Matt 9:22; Mark 5:34). And it will end with the Lord saying, "Come, you who are blessed of My Father, inherit the kingdom prepared for you from the foundation of the world" (Matt 25:34). That is the promise of the touch of Jesus.

ENDNOTES

[1] All Scripture quotations are from the NASB1995.

8
GOD IS OUR FOUNDATION

ED GALLAGHER

Blessed are those who hear the word of God and keep it!
(Luke 11:28)

* * *

It is a pleasure to dedicate an essay to a volume
honoring Barbara Dillon, an example of faithfulness
to everyone who knows her—faithfulness to her God and
her family, and faithfulness in her many years of service at
Heritage Christian University. Barbara, thank you for
your wonderful contributions to the mission of God!

* * *

I have done some stupid things in my life. Once at college,
I was in a club that participated in a soapbox derby on

campus, competing against other clubs. Somehow I got put in charge of our club's soapbox car one year, and somehow no one could find the car that had belonged to the club in previous years, or it had broken, or something. Anyway, I had to design a brand new car. That sort of thing would be a struggle for me now, but back in college, it wasn't just a challenge—it was quite impossible. The night before the race, I took a friend to a hardware store, where we purchased ... I don't know ... I think some ¾ inch plywood, some screws, and some wheels. We created a big, heavy box (not aerodynamic in the least), in which a man was supposed to ride down a hill—fast. Out of all our many failures, our biggest was the wheels, which were not secured to the vehicle well enough. I know, that sounds dangerous. But they weren't secured well enough even to be dangerous. As soon as our driver got in the car, the wheels popped off and the car just sat there on the road.

Let me say it again: that car had all kinds of problems —it was a long way from being a winner—but its biggest problem was the wheels, or, really, the way the wheels were attached to the frame. The wheels could not support the weight of the car and the driver. If the car had been perfect except for this one flaw, the result would have been the same. The car would not go.

Jesus tells a story about a couple fellows who both build houses, and both houses experienced the coming of a storm, but only one of the houses survived the storm. The difference, of course, was the foundation.

THE TWO BUILDERS

The story of the wise and foolish builders appears twice in our Bibles, once at the end of the Sermon on the Mount (Matt 7:24–27) and again as the conclusion of Luke's Sermon on the Plain (Luke 6:46–49). This lesson will focus on the version in Luke with some attention to the version in Matthew. In both locations, the parable serves as the conclusion to a major block of teaching from Jesus.

Though less familiar, the version in Luke makes the same basic point as the version in Matthew and contains a little more detail as to the good builder's foundation. We all remember the kid's song, "The wise man built his house upon the rock," which is based on Matthew's version of the parable. Luke's version actually does not use the terms "wise man" and "foolish man," but one man still builds his house on rock (Greek *petra*). This man "dug deep and laid the foundation on the rock. And when the flood arose, the stream beat vehemently against that house, and could not shake it, for it was founded on the rock" (6:48). The other fellow built his house "on the earth without a foundation," so that when "the stream beat vehemently" against his house, "immediately it fell. And the ruin of that house was great" (6:49).

Where I live in northwest Alabama, we know something about the floods rising and houses being threatened by a stream—or, in our case, the Tennessee River. For the past several years, we have had winters that set records for rainfall. A couple years ago, the Tennessee River in our area rose to over thirty feet, whereas flood stage is at about eighteen feet. Our local newspaper ran stories about people with flooded homes who had no flood insurance because they didn't live close enough to the river to be in a designated flood zone. Even with all our sophisticated weather-prediction technology, floods have caught people off guard. It can happen fast. It can be unexpected.

Why would somebody be so dumb as to build a house without a foundation, as described in Jesus's parable? Well, let me remind you of my soapbox car. I built a piece of junk because (a) I didn't know what I was doing, and (b) I didn't have time to learn. Part of the issue here is time, and effort. Notice what the good builder does: "he dug deep and laid the foundation on the rock." Of course, that is the better thing to do, but it also takes time and energy. It's a lot easier to just start building right there on the ground rather than digging deep. Let's change the metaphor. Sometimes I'll cook a meal for my family, and I'll have to cut up some vegetables, perhaps potatoes, maybe an onion. Anytime I do that, I have a little internal debate: "Do I want to spend a minute sharpening my knife? Maybe it's still sharp enough, since I did sharpen it before the last time I used it. But if it's not sharp enough, chopping vegetables is going to take longer. Plus, a dull knife is more dangerous than a sharp knife. If I end up cutting myself because I had to press harder on the dull knife, well, that's going to be a net loss. Better to just go ahead and sharpen the thing." Do you ever have debates with yourself like that? Sharpening a knife is a much different thing from building a house, but I can completely understand why someone might want to take the easy way out on some projects, cut some corners, save a little money, try to get done quicker.

There are a lot of times when we just want to take the easy way out. Do I want to put in the effort to being loving and respectful to my spouse? Do I want to invest in my kids right now, or just sit and read the paper or scroll through my feeds? I haven't read the Bible in a while, but I don't really get anything out of it, anyway. I should probably pray but I'm so tired.

Jesus is reminding us that the way of Jesus cannot be called "the easy way." It is a life of sacrifice, but it is also the only preparation for the coming storm.

THE COMING STORM

Jesus reminds us in this parable that the storm is coming, and no matter how you might try, you cannot avoid the storm. The man who wisely builds his house on the rock still faces the storm and that vehemently-beating stream, just like the man who foolishly builds without a secure foundation. But you can prepare for the storm, and proper preparation will ensure that the storm doesn't wipe out your house.

What kind of storm is Jesus talking about? We use this metaphor so frequently that we probably hardly think about it in the context of this parable. We know exactly what "the storms of life" are. When you have marital problems, that is a stormy season. When you have rebellious teenagers, that's a storm. You go through a storm when you lose your job, or you get a bad diagnosis, or a family member dies. In all such situations, you will find help in the teachings of Jesus. If you base your life on Jesus, if God is your foundation, you will make it through these storms with your house intact.

I don't think so. I don't mean that I doubt that the teachings of Jesus can provide guidance and security through life's difficulties. I just don't think that's what Jesus is talking about. What would that interpretation of the parable even mean? What would the house represent, in that case? Let's say you're having marital problems, and you base your life on the teachings of Jesus, then ... what? The marital problems will go away? Is that what it means that the house survives the storm? But, no, we can't really believe that. You might end up getting a divorce. If your spouse wants to leave, basing your life on Jesus's teachings is not necessarily going to prevent it. So what does it mean that the house survives the storm? Maybe that you come through your marital problems with your faith intact? But that would basically mean that if you base your life on the teachings of Jesus, then you will base your life on the teachings of Jesus. Or, think of it from the other side: are we supposed to believe that someone without Jesus will face more difficulties in these storms? In what way would that be? Jesus actually tells His disciples that they are going to face difficulties in life specifically because they are His disciples (Luke 6:22–23). I don't think the storm represents life's difficulties.

The storm is judgment. The parable is not about troublesome times during our lives, but about the end of our lives. Jesus is trying to get us ready to face the final storm, the big one. The only way to survive it is to base our lives on His teachings. Failure to do so will ensure the destruction of our house.

Remember that Luke has already introduced us to the teachings of John the Baptist, who warned that "One mightier than I is coming" (3:16). "His winnowing fan is in His hand, and He will thoroughly clean out His threshing floor, and gather the wheat into His barn; but the chaff He will burn with unquenchable fire" (3:17). This is a description of "the wrath to come" (3:7).

The storm of God's judgment is coming. There's only one way to prepare. Listen to what Jesus says—and do it!

HEARING AND DOING

> But be doers of the word, and not hearers only, deceiving yourselves. For if anyone is a hearer of the word and not a doer, he is like a man observing his natural face in a mirror; for he observes himself, goes away, and immediately forgets what kind of man he was. But he who looks into the perfect law of liberty and continues in it, and is not a forgetful hearer but a doer of the work, this one will be blessed in what he does (Jas 1:22–25).

The way Jesus tells it, the foolish builder is like a person who hears Jesus's words and does nothing about it (Luke

6:49). The wise builder is like a person who hears Jesus's words and puts them into practice. The difference is not that one heard the word and the other did not. They both heard. The difference is that only one of them enacted Jesus's words.

Now, of course, hearing is necessary, and the fact that you are reading a lesson like this shows your commitment to hearing the words of Jesus. I wonder how committed you are to doing them. Please, don't take offence. I don't mean that you're so much worse at doing what Jesus says than I am. I mean that what Jesus asks us to do is hard, and it is easier said (or heard) than done. I remember watching cooking shows when I was younger, and my mouth would water as I saw those chefs create magnificent meals, but never once did I actually go in the kitchen and prepare their recipe, and so I never ate one of those meals. If you want to eat the meal, hearing about it is not enough; you've got to cook it.

Before getting off "hearing," let me just say: our churches need to recommit to hearing the word of God. If God is our foundation (according to the title of this lesson), then we need to make it a point of emphasis to listen to what He has to say. I know, there are parts of the Bible that are hard to understand. But, look, these days, with how easy it is to own a Bible, with how many freely available study tools there are online (my favorites: Wikipedia and Google Maps), there is very little excuse for us not to at least make the attempt to read—or, rather, study —the Bible every day. Remember, the wise builder "dug deep and laid the foundation on the rock." Making the personal commitment to daily Bible study will do more to strengthen the church than just about anything else. After all, God gave His people Scripture to train them in righteousness (2 Tim 3:16).

Such training demands putting it in to practice, and that is what Jesus wanted to emphasize in His parable of the two builders. And, by the way, what I just said about how personal Bible study will strengthen the church— that's really true only if (let me say it once again: *only if*) we commit ourselves to putting into practice what we read. Jesus told this parable (whether in Matthew or Luke) after a major block of teaching material. So the most immediate application has to do with the very words He had just been telling people. When He says that the wise builder "hears My sayings and does them," He means the sayings that He had just spoken—stuff like "love your enemies" (Luke 6:27) and "turn the other cheek" (6:29) and the Golden Rule (6:31) and "judge not" (6:37) and "forgive" (6:37). This is the kind of thing that will see you through the coming storm, but you've got to put it into practice. Because if you don't ... well, don't say that Jesus didn't warn you.

LESSONS LEARNED

God is our foundation. The word of God is our foundation. Hearing and doing the word of God is our foundation. These statements do not contradict; they are mutually reinforcing. Just as Jesus said, "If you love me, keep my commandments" (John 14:15), so also we could say that if God is our foundation, that means—at least, in part—that we must trust and obey Him. Of course, we do not earn salvation (Eph 2:8–9), and obedience has nothing to do with accumulating merit; it has everything to do with trusting Him. As the brother of Jesus says, hearing without doing is demonic (Jas 2:19).

9

EXEGESIS OF 1 THESSALONIANS
4:9−12

MICHAEL JACKSON

Donfried states it best when he says, "The renewed interest in 1 Thessalonians during the last two decades has been extraordinary" (3). Any examination of the current literature is daunting to even the most studious biblical scholar. Perhaps more puzzling, however, is the variation of viewpoints that have developed (and even *are* developing) regarding this text. While this research purports to examine only a small portion of the Thessalonian correspondence, the expansion of ideas regarding the epistle has a direct effect upon the interpretation of such a pericope. As with any research of this kind, it is best to start at the beginning: a general introduction.

GENERAL INTRODUCTION

It must be stated that for a research of this size to accomplish its goals, some things must be assumed. It is not to be assumed that the writer has *not* examined many of the various arguments, but that he *has* scrutinized them and come to some conclusions based on evidence. For this particular introduction authorship, date and occasion, form and structure, and eschatology will form the basis of these assumptions.

AUTHORSHIP

The Thessalonian letters claim to be written by Paul, Silvanus, and Timothy (1 and 2 Thess 1:1). Internal and external evidence points to a strong Pauline influence, if not total authorship (Morris 15). Bruce observes that the authenticity of Pauline authorship of both letters has been questioned from time to time (xxxiii). Bruce notes that F.C. Baur was a pioneer in the argument against Pauline authorship of 1 Thessalonians (xxxiii), and more recent scholarship has given more detail, expounding on the fact that Karl Schrader was the earlier cynic (Green 55). It is important to notice that both scholars mentioned are from the 19th century A.D. This and much other evidence leads Wanamaker to exclaim that "no contemporary scholars of repute seem to doubt the authentic Pauline character of the letter" (17). For this research, Pauline authorship is assumed based on the current evidence.

DATE AND OCCASION

Most scholarship places the letter of 1 Thessalonians shortly after the evangelization of the church there (Bruce xxxiv). In Acts 17:1–15 we have the account of the establishment of the church in Thessalonica, in which the current proconsul is mentioned as being Gallio. Gallio is mentioned in the Delphi inscription which dates him as being proconsul sometime between 50–52 A.D. (Bruce xxxiv). For this research, the general date of 50–52 A.D. will suffice.

FORM AND STRUCTURE

Stott sees correctly that there are two main portions to Paul's letter, which are common in many of his writings— 1. Narrative (1:1–3:13), and 2. Exhortation (4:1–5:28). While there are many different opinions on the structure of 1 Thessalonians, most of these are related to the misunderstanding of the unity of the epistle (cf. Richard 11ff, Stott 19). While this may seem a bit oversimplified, for this research it is important to note that Paul did have a two-fold reason for writing the Thessalonians (conversation and instruction) just as modern writers have in their correspondence.

THE ESCHATOLOGY OF THE THESSALONIANS

Perhaps the most obvious theme in the Thessalonian communication is the *Parousia* or second coming of Jesus.

Malherbe states, "It is this pervasive eschatological dimension in the letter that gives the Thessalonian community its special character" (79). Thessalonians presents the first written evidence of the use of *Parousia* for the coming of Christ (Bruce xxxvi). The Thessalonian church was in its infancy and did not have much time to learn from its missionaries the details of the second coming. It is understandable that they were curious about those who had already passed away (4:13–18) and about the timing of the Advent (5:1–11). Paul thus addresses their questions. For this research, it is assumed that eschatology was a major concern for the Thessalonians.

LITERARY CONTEXT

1 Thessalonians is obviously a letter. But what type of letter? In the case of 1 Thessalonians, a correct understanding of the "diverse methodological approaches" can illustrate the incompatibility of the interpretations that are developed in their use (Donfried 4). For instance, some claim 1 Thessalonians to be an *apologia* against Paul's enemies (Frame 12ff). Such authors then see *everything* included in the letter through that understanding. It, in a sense, biases them against any other understanding. While the analysis of Paul's literary style in Thessalonians is of great import, we must remain hesitant to insist that an epistolary or rhetorical analysis determines *all* of the intentions of the author (Donfried 5). Thus, our first task is not to overanalyze the text for sub-sub-sub-sub structures, but to try to understand it in its original context to

its original audience. Thus, the literary context of Thessalonians is one of friendly letter and exhortation (cf. Hendriksen 12).

LIMITS OF THE TEXT

The strong contrastive περι δε (now concerning) separates our text (1 Thess 4:9–12) from the rest of the letter. It serves as a natural change from the exhortation in 4:1–8. The use of εχω in verses 9 and 12 serves as nice grammatical bookends to indicate the open and close of this particular paraenesis. These factors along with the introduction of a new subject beginning with περι δε in verse 13 indicate that verses 9–12 are to be taken as a group.

ROLE OF THE TEXT IN THESSALONIANS

The instruction on brotherly love in 4:9–12 might seem strange sandwiched between exhortation on sexual immorality and the *Parousia*. In fact, Weatherly comments that Paul's tone is "remarkably different" from the preceding material (140). Martin correctly remarks, however, that this is "reminiscent of the changes in topic found in 1 Corinthians" and "all of this is consistent with the character of paraenesis and can be seen in other authors as well" (133). The fact is that in this paraenesis, Paul changes his topic to deal with specific problems of the Thessalonians rather than writing in an essay type format (Gaventa 59). It is natural to shift subjects in a list of exhortations. If the exhortations are multiple, then so are the written subject changes!

TEXTUAL ANALYSIS

The text of 1 Thessalonians 4:9–12 is problematic in only a very few instances. In verse 9, NA27 lists variants of εχομεν and ειχομεν in place of the more awkward εχετε (535). In spite of the later manuscripts' easier reading, the earlier manuscript tradition (ℵ and A) seems to support the harder construction. In any case, the sense of the passage is not altered. NA27 follows the same textual tradition in verse 11 when it includes ιδιαις (although only in brackets) when describing "one's own hands" (535). These variants are interesting, but make very little bearing on the intended outcome of the passage at hand. NA27's reading is to be accepted.

TRANSLATION

A proper translation of 1 Thessalonians 4:9–12 would be,

> But concerning brotherly love, you do not have need *for us* to write to you, for you yourselves are taught by God to love one another. For indeed you do this to all the brethren who are in all of Macedonia. We urge you, brethren, to abound more *in brotherly love* and to aspire to lead a quiet life and to tend to your own business and to work with your own hands, just as we commanded you, in order that you may conduct yourselves properly

towards outsiders and you may not have need of anything.

OUTLINE

The following is a proper outline of the paraenesis:
1 Thessalonians 4:9–10a Paralipsis on brotherly love

- 4:9a Paralipsis regarding love—"you don't need us to write to you"
- 4:9b Reason—"you are taught by God to love one another"
- 4:10a Reason #2 (perhaps progressive)—"you are already doing this" (Richard 210)

1 Thessalonians 4:10b–11 Daily living in light of love

- 4:10b Command—"we urge you, brethren"
- 4:10c Series of Exhortations—"to love more"
- 4:11a Series of Exhortations—"to aspire to live a quiet life"
- 4:11b Series of Exhortations—"to mind your own business"
- 4:11c Series of Exhortations—"to work with your own hands"

1 Thessalonians 4:12 The aim of this instruction

- 4:12a Purpose and Result—"that you may walk worthily toward outsiders"

- 4:12b Purpose and Result—"that you may not have need of anything"

This structure is certainly not without dispute! Frame and others disconnect 4:9–10a from 4:10b–12 even more sharply, giving them distinctive purposes (157–9). While a case for this understanding might appear even logical based on the topics covered, these verses are grammatically connected and the instruction on idleness is clearly connected to brotherly love (Wanamaker 159). It is significant that the paraenesis is so neatly organized, giving it the clarity and force Paul was trying to convey to the Thessalonians.

WORD AND CONCEPT ANALYSIS

In verse 9 Paul introduces the word φιλαδελφια, a word used only six times in the New Testament. BAGD points out that the word usually connoted a literal sense of love for a blood brother or sister (858). However, in the New Testament, this love is figuratively applied to the love between those of the Christian faith (858). Marshall sees φιλαδελφια as mutual love contrasted with αγαπη or "unrequited" love (114). Best says, "To the Christian, **brother** is not merely a metaphor but a reality; since…kinship had often been broken at conversion they appreciated more firmly the ties of spiritual kinship" (172). Thus, Paul's instruction takes on a specifically communal role with regards to the Thessalonians (Jewett 75).

In verse 10 Paul possibly introduces an entirely new

word into the Greek language. Θεοδιδακτος and its meaning are made complex because of the use of the present tense (Richard 210). This is its only use in the New Testament, and all other occurrences of the word post-date this one. This has led some scholars to contend that this is a totally new word. TDNT correctly defines the word as "taught of God" generally, without giving any specifics (3:121). The exegetical question, however, is how the Thessalonians are *presently* taught of God. Green is right to suggest that whether this teaching was the indwelling Holy Spirit or the example of Christ on the cross, "the command *to love one another* was a hallmark of Jesus's teaching" (205). Paul does not specify how they were taught, just that they "already had in hand the teaching they needed" (Green 205).

CONTEXT AND COMMENT

Verse 9. The major point of conflict in verse 9 among scholars has little to do with the content of Paul's teaching, and much to do with the context of his teaching. Some commentators fervently defend the position that the "Thessalonians had written Paul expressly for advice in this matter" (Frame 157). Others, however, see that "it is unlikely that, whether orally or in writing, they would have used such general phraseology as: 'What should we do about brotherly love'" (Bruce 89). Whichever viewpoint one accepts, the teaching is still the matter at hand.

Paul uses a figure of speech called *paralipsis* to introduce the subject of brotherly love to the Thessalonians, "whereby an 'orator pretends to pass over something which he, in fact, mentions'" (Richard 210). Paul's instruction is therefore gentle, but not passive. He recognized the need for the Thessalonians to love even more, but they were actively already practicing love.

The reasons that Paul states for not having to instruct them on the matter occur in two γαρ phrases in 9b and 10a. In the first phrase, it is stated that they are "taught by God", a concept examined earlier. This divine communication and relationship was mentioned by Jesus in John 6:45 and would have been strong grounds for the Thessalonians to recognize that the call for love was much higher than even the apostles.

Verse 10. The second reason advances upon the first one (Morris 129). Not only had they been divinely taught to love, they had already been practicing it! "His use of the continuous present tense indicates their habitual attitude" (Morris 129). Paul was not trying to say that the Thessalonians didn't practice love, but he was gently persuading them to continue in that love and to abound even more.

Wanamaker appropriately remarks that 10b "could be taken with what follows, suggesting a new theme", but that "it seems more likely that...he is referring back to their love" (161–2). In fact, verses 9–12 are so closely linked grammatically; one could hardly make a strong case to separate them. It is at this point that Paul begins a string of four infinitive constructions dependent upon the exhortation παρακαλουμεν.

The first of the exhortations is for the Thessalonians to abound even more in love for one another, and there is "no limit to the extent...to which love may be exercised" (Best 174). Morris notes, "The love of which Paul writes is intensely practical" and "that is the quality for which he looks" (130).

Verse 11. The second of Paul's instructions is to be ambitious to be quiet! Bruce recognizes that it is "commonly supposed that undue eschatological excitement had induced a restless tendency...and made them disinclined to attend to their ordinary business" (91). This viewpoint is not without debate. For example, Green sees this whole section through Roman politics and the patron/client system (210). He sees this as a call for Christians to stay out of political affairs (210). While it is possible not to see the cause of the Thessalonian unrest in their eschatological nature, the burden of proof falls upon Green to take the extra step in establishing Paul's address of anything political. It is best to view the eschatological nature of the Thessalonians and the politics of Rome as *possible* reasons for their problem.

The third exhortation, or possibly the continuation of the second, is for the Thessalonians to mind their own business (Richard 211, Wanamaker 162). This expression occurs only here in the New Testament but is very common in Greek literature (Morris 131). It is clear that Paul wants the Thessalonians to put their attention where it belongs (Morris 132).

The fourth and final infinitival clause instructs the Thessalonians to work with their own hands. Brotherly love demanded that they have "sober and industrious habits", which they had already been told (Bruce 91). Paul had indeed set the pace in this respect (2:9), and he expected the Thessalonians to follow suit.

Verse 12. Finally in this instruction, Paul gives the aim of all that he has told them. First of all, his purpose and intended result is that they may conduct themselves properly toward outsiders. Paul did not want any quarrels or "new waves of oppression" in Thessalonica (Wanamaker 164). Rather, the Thessalonians should conduct themselves in a way that brings no reason for the outside community to be stirred up.

Secondly, Paul did not want the Thessalonians to become a burden or dependency on anyone or anything. Paul does not want the Christian community to become "a parasite on society" (Marshall 117). The Thessalonians should provide for their own needs so that they would not have to search elsewhere to fulfill them.

APPLICATION

Modern Christians that have love, but don't lead quiet lives, mind their own business or work to support themselves are a bit contradictory to the outside world. They stain the reputation of the Church and end up hungry and destitute by wasting their time away in idleness. Christians need to learn to love and live in such a way that brings honor and self-sufficiency to themselves and the church.

APPENDIX A: PREACHING/TEACHING OUTLINE

"Instruction on Daily Christian Living"

Introduction

I live in a world of isolation. I can write letters through e-mail, buy stamps on the internet, pay all my bills online, see all the world on my TV screen, and even buy groceries on the 'net, all without ever seeing or interacting with another human being.

I live in a world of loud-living. When I do cut on my television or get onto the internet, all I see are those who stand out in the crowd—the stars with the most money, the most immorality, the loudest mouths. The raunchier the content, the more popular it becomes.

I live in a world of gossip and meddling. Since I don't get out much, your problems become my daily fodder. In today's world, I don't even have to leave my house to read about you and gossip about you. We have blogs, e-mail, and chatrooms for that. But when I do get out, that's really all that there is to talk about. What else can you talk about if you aren't talking about other people?

I live in a world of laziness. Big surprise, huh. After all that I've said so far, you wonder how I have even been able to retain my muscle mass. My couch is my home, my computer chair is my friend, and my fulfillment is in my pleasure.

I need to be taught!

This morning, I want to talk to you about a similar

people in a similar time who needed a similar teaching: The Thessalonians.

First of all,

We must strive to love more (4:9–10)

Expl. → Even though the Thessalonians were known for love, Paul says love more!

Expl. → What kind of "love" is this brotherly love?

- Genuine (Rom 12:9–10)
- Continuing (Heb 13:1)
- From the **obedience** to the truth (1 Pet 1:22)
- Essential (1 John 4:20–21)

Appl. → We cannot love our brothers and sisters in Christ enough. Even when our love is witnessed by everyone in Alabama, Paul would say "love more!"

After his instruction on love, Paul tells us that

We must strive to live "quiet lives" (4:11a)

Illus. → We all know the folks that can't keep their cool at the ball games... After little league games they wait to chew on the umpire's ear, they regularly taunt opposing teams and individuals, and they can't seem to keep their temper down... I have a personal example of this...

Expl. → The Bible is very poetic on this point (OT— Prov 17:1, Lam 3:26, NT—1 Tim 2:2, Women—1 Pet 3:4)

Appl. → We need to always be conscious of where our ambition is taking us. Are we aspiring to quietness, living each day to the glory of God and his Church, or are we controlling our ambitions at all?

Thirdly, Paul says that

We must strive to mind our own business (4:11b)

Expl. → This is perhaps the earliest known usage of our idiom "Mind your own business!" It literally means to "do one's own things."

Illus. → The denominational preacher Dwight L. Moody walked down a Chicago street one day and saw a man leaning against a lamppost. The evangelist gently put his hand on the man's shoulder and asked the stranger if he was a Christian. The fellow raised his fists and angrily exclaimed, "Mind your own business!" "I'm sorry if I've offended you," said Moody, "but to be very frank, that is my business!"

If we have become part of God's family in Christ, then the spiritual health of others automatically becomes our business. But that is not what we are talking about, and neither is it usually *what* we talk about!!!!

Appl. → Our daily Christian walk does not afford us the time nor the energy to get involved in the worldly affairs of others. Gossip, idle talk, and meddling in the affairs of others are all condemned by Paul.

The last thing Paul instructs here is that

We must strive to work with our own hands (4:11c)

Expl. → Paul said it best himself when he said, "If a man is not willing to work, let him not eat" (2 Thess 3:10) and "But if any provide not for his own, and especially for those of his own house, he hath denied the faith, and is worse than an infidel" (1 Tim 5:8).

Expl. → Not only is this practical, but it is Christian! (see the command in 3:10)

Appl. → We must endeavor to work hard and teach our

children to work hard. We don't just work because it gives us money or food, but because it is a Christian command and it serves a respectable purpose.

CONCLUSION

The whole point of Paul's instruction is summed up in verse 12. When we fall into the trap of lacking love, living loudly, meddling in others' affairs, and being lazy—then we ruin our reputation. People on the outside see our actions and they form a view of us and the church.

Changing this community and this world for Christ begins on the individual, daily level!!! When we lose this basic focus then we set the church up for ridicule, and we aren't even able to provide for our basic needs. On the other hand, if we live like Paul teaches here, then we bring glory, honor, praise, and people to the kingdom of our Lord and Savior Jesus Christ.

What will your aim be this morning?

WORKS CITED

(BAGD) Bauer, Walter, William F. Arndt, F. Wilbur Gingrich, and Frederick W. Danker. *A Greek-English Lexicon of the New Testament and other Early Christian Literature*. 2nd ed. Chicago: The University of Chicago Press, 1979.

Best, Ernest. *Black's New Testament Commentary: The First and Second Epistles to the Thessalonians*. Peabody, MA: Hendrickson, 1986.

Bruce, F.F. *1 and 2 Thessalonians*. Word Biblical Commentary 45. Nashville: Nelson Reference and Electronic, 1982.

Donfried, Karl P., and Johannes Beutler, eds. *The Thessalonians Debate: Methodological Discord or Methodological Synthesis?* Grand Rapids: Eerdmans, 2000.

Frame, James Everett. *A Critical and Exegetical Commentary on the Epistles of St. Paul to the Thessalonians.* Edinburgh: T. and T. Clark, 1988.

Gaventa, Beverly Roberts. *First and Second Thessalonians.* Interpretation. Louisville: John Knox, 1998.

Green, Gene L. *The Letters to the Thessalonians.* Pillar New Testament Commentary. Grand Rapids: Eerdmans, 2002.

Hendriksen, William, and Simon J. Kistemaker. *New Testament Commentary: Exposition of Thessalonians, the Pastorals, and Hebrews.* Grand Rapids: Baker Books, 1995.

The Holy Bible: New Revised Standard Version. Oxford: Oxford University Press, 2001.

Jewett, Robert. *The Thessalonian Correspondence: Pauline Rhetoric and Millenarian Piety.* Philadelphia: Fortress, 1986.

Malherbe, Abraham J. *Paul and the Thessalonians: The Philosopic Tradition of Pastoral Care.* Philadelphia: Fortress, 1987.

Marshall, I. Howard. *New Century Bible Commentary: 1 and 2 Thessalonians.* Grand Rapids: Eerdmans, 1983.

Martin, D. Michael. *1, 2 Thessalonians.* The New American Commentary 33. Nashville: Broadman and Holman, 1995.

Morris, Leon. *The First and Second Epistles to the Thessa-*

lonians. New International Commentary on the New Testament. Rev. ed. Grand Rapids: Eerdmans, 1991.

(NA27) *Novum Testamentum Graece*. Stuttgart, Germany: Deutsche Bibelgesellschaft, 1999.

Richard, Earl J. *First and Second Thessalonians*. Sacra Pagina Series 11. Collegeville, MN: Liturgical, 1995.

Smith, Abraham. *Comfort One Another: Reconstructing the Rhetoric and Audience of 1 Thessalonians*. Louisville: John Knox, 1995.

Stott, John. *The Gospel and the End of Time*. The Bible Speaks Today Series. Downers Grove, IL: InterVarsity, 1991.

(TDNT) Kittel, Gerhard. *Theological Dictionary of the New Testament*. Trans. and ed. Geoffrey W. Bromiley, 10 vols. Grand Rapids: Eerdmans, 1964–1976.

Wanamaker, Charles A. *The Epistles to the Thessalonians: A Commentary on the Greek Text*. New International Greek New Testament. Grand Rapids: Eerdmans, 1990.

Weatherly, Jon A. *The College Press NIV Commentary: 1 and 2 Thessalonians*. Joplin, MO: College Press, 1996.

10

FEARLESS FAITH

BRIANA BUTLER

Throughout the Bible, we are given examples of women with fearless faith. We read about Deborah and Rahab, who were bold and courageous, and about Hannah, who prayed amidst difficult times and never gave up hope. These women are well-known for their faith and dedication to the Lord in times of trouble. However, there are women in the Bible who are only mentioned briefly but had a tremendous impact on those around them and for generations after. These women are faithful, gentle leaders behind the scenes but deserve the recognition often given to those more familiar names.

In 2 Timothy 1:5, Paul writes to Timothy about his sincere faith, "a faith that dwelt first in your grandmother Lois and your mother Eunice and now, I am sure, dwells in you as well" (ESV). While this is the only instance of Lois and Eunice mentioned by name in the Bible, these two women had fearless faith and instilled their knowledge into young Timothy. Timothy grew up to be a faithful missionary and traveling companion with Paul. He was known for his genuine confidence and trust in the Lord, which undoubtedly came from the time spent with his mother and grandmother. We can infer that Lois and Eunice did not simply tell Timothy what to do but led by their daily actions. As shown by Lois and Eunice, genuine faith can inspire others and encourage them to maintain a lifelong dedication to the cause of Christ.

Manoah's wife, the mother of Samson, is another example of a quiet servant with fearless faith. While she is never listed by name, the entire chapter of Judges 13 is dedicated to her faith. She was barren but was visited multiple times by a man known only as "the angel of the Lord", who told her she would bear a son. After the angel of the Lord appeared to Manoah and his wife for the last time, Manoah said to his wife, "We shall surely die, for we have seen God" (Judg 13:22). Manoah's wife instead gave Manoah several reasons why they would not die and why he could be reassured of this. Her faith did not waiver, and she "bore a son and called his name Samson" (Judg 13:24). When we model genuine faith, others take notice. Manoah's wife relied on her faith to reassure Manoah of God's promise for them and their child.

These examples show women who led quietly and gently. They made a tremendous impact for the cause of Christ through their knowledge and gentle spirit. They trusted God and ensured their loved ones had the same strong faith. Paul writes to Titus in Titus 3:1–2, "Remind them to be submissive to rulers and authorities, to be obedient, to be ready for every good work, to speak evil of no one, to avoid quarreling, to be gentle, and to show perfect courtesy to all people." No one embodies a fearless faith and gentle spirit quite like Barbara Dillon. She is zealous for the work of the Lord and enthusiastic for His cause. Often opting to be out of the spotlight, Barbara shines bright as an ever-present encouragement to her fellow Christians.

11
BETTER

JAMIE COX

The book of Hebrews, though the author is unknown, offers us a glimpse of how much better life under the new covenant is. Let us look briefly at what is better now than under the old law.

Hebrews 1:4 tells us that Jesus is better than the angels. Though both Jesus and the angles are living in heaven, Jesus purged our sins, sits on the right hand of the Majesty on high and "has by inheritance obtained a more excellent name than they." Angels are only "ministering spirits sent forth to minister for those who will inherit salvation" (Heb 1:14). Jesus Christ is the Son of God whom God has given power and dominion over all the earth and hath made His enemies His footstool (Heb 1:13). Jesus allowed Himself to be made lower than the angels so that He might suffer temptation. His suffering makes Him better "to aid those who are tempted (Heb 2:18).

Jesus is better than Moses. Jesus was a prophet like Moses but as Moses stated in Deuteronomy 18:15–19

> The Lord your God will raise up for you a prophet like me from among you, for your brothers—it is to him you shall listen—just as you desired of the Lord your God at Horeb on the day of the assembly, when you said, "Let me not hear again the voice of the Lord my God or see this great fire any more, lest I die." And the Lord said to me, "They are right in what they have spoken. I will raise up for them a prophet like you from among their brothers And I will put my words in his mouth, and he shall speak to them all that I command him. And whoever will not listen to my words that he shall speak in my name, I myself will require it of him.

Moses foretold of a great and better prophet that would be sent. Moses did not enter the Promised Land because of his disobedience to God at Kadesh (Num 20:1–12). Jesus however was faithful in all things and "... in Him there is no sin" (1 John 3:5, Heb 4:15).

The new covenant is better than the old covenant. The old covenant could not be kept perfectly. The new covenant does not require man to be perfect but allows for the forgiveness of sins. The old law made nothing perfect. The sacrifices were rolled forward and were not truly forgiven until the death of Christ on the cross. The new covenant gives man "a better hope through which we draw near to God" (Heb 7:19). The new covenant is written on the minds and hearts of man not on tablets of stones as the old covenant had been written. The new covenant is more spiritual than the old covenant which was more physical. The old covenant was only between God and the Israelites. The new covenant is between God and all those who accept Him regardless of nationality. The new covenant is established on better promises (Heb 8:6).

The tabernacle under the new covenant is better. The tabernacle under the old law was made out of cloth and contained items that were simply symbolic. Only the priest could enter the tabernacle and only the high priest once a year could enter the Holiest of All. It was only after he had offered sacrifices for his sins and the sins of the people could he enter. The tabernacle under the new law is not made with hand of this creation (Heb 9:11). Christ offered not the blood of bulls and goats but His own blood. He does not have to keep offering a sacrifice yearly only once did He need to offer Himself.

The new covenant required that a death must occur to put an end to the old testament. This death was the death of Christ on the cross. As the Old Testament was filled with blood of those animals that died so the New Testament is filled with the blood that Christ shed on the cross (Heb 9–10).

The new covenant ends the need for animal sacrifices and gives us better law that can be lived more perfectly. We are allowed to enter the new covenant regardless of nationality simply by obeying the will of Jesus Christ, the author of eternal salvation (Heb 5:9).

Jesus is a better High Priest. Christ is more compassionate than the high priest appointed by men (Heb 4:13–14). High priests under the Mosaic Law had to offer sacrifices for themselves first because of their sins. Since Christ is sinless, His sacrifice was for others not Himself. High priests were only high priest till their death. Jesus is a High Priest forever. There is no "changing of the guard" (Heb 7:24).

Jesus was a better sacrifice. He was pure, spotless, without blemish.

Jesus Christ, the Son of God, provides a better way of life to those that will follow Him. He is greater than the angels in heaven. He was sinless while on earth yet suffered as we do and learned obedience and has compassion to aid us. Jesus provides us with a better way of communicating with our Father in that He sits on His right hand and intercedes on our behalf (Heb 7:25).

Because we live under a better covenant, we have a greater need to live holding fast to the faith which we have in Christ Jesus (Heb 10:23). The better covenant allows us to live a life that is closer to Him in that He is our intercessor and gave His blood for us. We need to offer our lives to Him and be a living sacrifice for Him (Rom 12:1).

By living a better life under the better covenant, we have a better promise of a heavenly home (Heb 10:34). A better life involves not forgetting what has been done for us by Jesus's death. A better life involves not losing faith and hope during difficult times. A better life is considering "one another in order to stir up love and good works" (Heb 10:24). A better life is "not forsaking the assembling of ourselves together ... but exhorting one another" (Hebrews 10:25). A better life is enduring and pressing on to receive the promise of an everlasting eternal home with Him in heaven.

This better life is obtained by having faith that those who have gone on before us have had. Abel offered a more excellent sacrifice because of his faith in God. Enoch did not see death because of his faith in God but was taken from this earth without death. Noah prepared an ark and was saved from the flood due to his faith in God. Abraham left his home and sojourned to a foreign country and a promised land because of his faith in God. Sarah bore Isaac after childbearing years because of her faith in God. Faith in God caused Moses's parents to hid him in a basket on the water. Moses refused to be called the son of Pharaoh's daughter because of his faith. The children of Israel were lead across the Red Sea on dry ground because of faith. By faith, Rahab was saved when the walls of Jericho fell on the seventh day of marching (Heb 12).

Pleasing God is having faith in Him. Knowing Him and obeying Him through faith God will reward those that seek Him. Will you have the better resurrection because of your faith in God?

Scripture Index

CREDITS

1978, 1984, 2011 by Biblica, Inc.™ Used by permission of Zondervan. All rights reserved worldwide. www.zondervan.com The "NIV" and "New International Version" are trademarks registered in the United States Patent and Trademark Office by Biblica, Inc.®

Scripture quotations marked HCSB are been taken from the Holman Christian Standard Bible®, Copyright © 1999, 2000, 2002, 2003 by Holman Bible Publishers. Used by permission. Holman Christian Standard Bible®, Holman CSB®, and HCSB® are federally registered trademarks of Holman Bible Publishers.

Select scripture quotations are from The Authorized (King James) Version. Rights in the Authorized Version in the United Kingdom are vested in the Crown. Reproduced by permission of the Crown's patentee, Cambridge University Press.

Select scripture quotations are from the ESV® Bible (The Holy Bible, English Standard Version®), copyright © 2001 by Crossway, a publishing ministry of Good News Publishers. Used by permission. All rights reserved.

Select scripture quotations are from Revised Standard Version of the Bible, copyright © 1946, 1952, and 1971 National Council of the Churches of Christ in the United States of America. Used by permission. All rights reserved worldwide.

HERITAGE LEGACY SERIES

The Heritage Legacy Series follows the longstanding academic tradition of the *Festschrift*, a collection of essays in recognition of a respected colleague. Biblically, it embodies the principles of giving honor to whom honor is due and esteeming godly servants for their work. Heritage Christian University Press is happy to show appreciation to those who have blessed Heritage Christian University and the church in countless ways.

Things Most Surely Believed: Festschrift for Charlie Wayne Kilpatrick. Heritage Legacy Series. Edited by the Staff of Heritage Christian University Press. Florence, AL: Heritage Christian University Press, 2021.

Serving the Lord: A Festschrift for Freddie Patrick Moon and Janet Stewart Moon. Heritage Legacy Series. Edited by the

Staff of Heritage Christian University Press. Florence, AL: Heritage Christian University Press, 2022.

Fighting the Good Fight: A Festschrift for Bill Bagents. Heritage Legacy Series. Edited by the Staff of Heritage Christian University Press. Florence, AL: Heritage Christian University Press, 2022.

A Gentle and Quiet Spirit: A Festschrift for Barbara A. Dillon. Heritage Legacy Series. Edited by the Staff of Heritage Christian University Press. Florence, AL: Heritage Chris-tian University Press, 2023.

ALSO BY HERITAGE CHRISTIAN UNIVERSITY PRESS

Redrawing the Blueprints for the Early Church: Historical Ecclesiology in and around the Stone-Campbell Movement

by John Young

Berean Study Series. Edited by Ed Gallagher and Bill Bagents

Clothed in Christ: A How to Guide

Cloud of Witnesses: Ancient Stories of Faith

The Ekklesia of Christ: Becoming the People of God

For the Glory of God: Christ and the Church in Ephesians

Instructions for Living: The Ten Commandments

Led by God's Spirit: A Practical Study of Galatians 5:22–26

Majesty and Mercy: God Through the Eyes of Isaiah

Visions of Grace: Stories from Scripture

What Real Christianity Looks Like: A Study on the Parables

Cypress Bible Study Series. By Ed Gallagher

The Book of Exodus: Explorations in Christian Theology

The Gospel of Luke: Explorations in Christian Scripture

The Sermon on the Mount: Explorations in Christian Practice

Heritage Christian Leadership Institute Series

Corrupt Communication: Myths at Target Church Leaders
by Bill Bagents and Laura S. Bagents

Counseling for Church Leaders: A Practical Guide
by Bill Bagents and Rosemary Snodgrass

Lead Like the Lord: Lessons in Leadership from Jesus
by W. Kirk Brothers

Heritage Legacy Series. Edited by the Staff of Heritage
Christian University Press.

Fighting the Good Fight: A Festschrift for Bill Bagents

A Gentle and Quiet Spirit: A Festschrift for Barbara A. Dillon

*Serving the Lord: A Festschrift for Freddie Patrick Moon and
Janet Stewart Moon*

Things Most Surely Believed: Festschrift for Charlie Wayne Kilpatrick

CYPRESS

To see full catalog of Heritage Christian University Press and its imprint Cypress Publications, visit www.hcu.edu/publications.